Judaism

A SHORT HISTORY

'It is terse, concise, well written and gives the reader the basic facts he or she might want to know.'

JULIA NEUBERGER in *Theology*

'The book presents complex areas in intelligible language'

CHRISTINE PILKINGTON in the *Canterbury Cathedral Chronicle*

'Very useful for non-Jewish readers'

RON LEWIS in *World Faiths Encounter*

'Dr Dan and Mrs Lavinia Cohn-Sherbok rise to the challenge of squeezing more than 3,000 years of Jewish history into 148 pages.'

CHARLES H. MIDDLEBURGH in the *Expository Times*

'An authoritative and comprehensive study'

Network

'. . . keep[s] up a lively narrative without becoming a mere catalogue of names and events . . . I can heartily recommend it'

LESLIE GRIFFITHS in the *Methodist Recorder*

Judaism

A SHORT HISTORY

Lavinia and Dan Cohn-Sherbok

ONEWORLD

OXFORD

JUDAISM: A SHORT HISTORY

Oneworld Publications
(Sales and Editorial)
185 Banbury Road
Oxford OX2 7AR
England
http://www.oneworld-publications.com

Oneworld Publications
(US Marketing Office)
160 N. Washington St.
4th Floor, Boston
MA 02114
USA

ISBN 1–85168–206–6

Cover design by Design Deluxe, Bath
Printed and bound in England by Clays Ltd, St Ives plc

CONTENTS

NOTE ON ABBREVIATIONS IN DATES

Throughout this book the abbreviations BC (Before Christ) and AD (Anno Domini, In the Year of Our Lord) have been replaced with the more widely accepted BCE (Before Common, or Christian, Era) and CE (Common, or Christian, Era).

1 THE MIDDLE EASTERN BACKGROUND

1. CANAAN AND ITS NEIGHBOURS

A person is Jewish if he or she has a Jewish mother. Although it is possible to convert to Judaism, Jewishness is not primarily a question of belief: it is quite possible to be a Jewish Christian or a Jewish Muslim. Biological descent rather than religious conviction is the crucial criterion. Jewishness is passed from mother to child through the generations and, with relatively few exceptions, Jews are born rather than made. Therefore, in examining the history of Judaism, we are not primarily studying the history of Jewish thought; instead, we are looking at the story of the Jewish people.

The Jewish people believe themselves to be descended from a Semitic tribe that dwelt in the land of Canaan. The biblical figure of Abraham is regarded as the tribal ancestor. According to the book of Genesis, Abraham left the Mesopotamian city of Ur and moved to Haran, and he was then commanded to take his family to the land of Canaan. It was promised that he would become the father of a great nation and that his descendants would be more numerous than the stars of Heaven and the grains of sand upon the sea-shore; they would inherit Canaan and it would be their rightful territory for ever.

The land of Canaan is normally understood to be an extensive area in the Eastern Mediterranean encompassing most of modern Israel, Jordan and Syria. In the third millennium BCE, the early Bronze Age, the great powers of the Middle East were the Old Kingdom of Egypt, the successive imperial states of Mesopotamia in the east, the land of the

Hittites in the north and the various independent city states that extended up the Mediterranean coast. There seems to have been considerable cultural unity between the coastal cities, although there was also commercial contact with both Egypt and Mesopotamia. This equilibrium seems to have been disturbed at the end of the millennium by invading groups of Asiatic nomads known as the Amurru or Amorites.

Eventually the city states managed to drive the Amurru back and re-establish themselves. In Mesopotamia the great powers of Assyria and Babylon competed with each other, spreading their domains and exerting their influence over particular cities such as Mari on the Euphrates, Aleppo and Ugarit. Egypt continued to maintain commercial links with the coastal cities as far north as Byblos. Meanwhile, outside the fortified cities, the nomadic Amurru tribes wandered with their herds and flocks through the hill and desert country. It is almost certainly to this period, after 1900 BCE, that the patriarchal records of the book of Genesis belong.

The land the Jewish people believe to be their inheritance has four main geographical divisions. On the west is the coastal plain, which provided an easy line of communication from north to south. West of the River Jordan lies the hill country, with the region of Galilee in the north, Ephraim in the centre and Judah to the south. The hill country is broken up by plains and fertile valleys, and to the south lies the Negeb desert. Further east is a great cleft through which the River Jordan flows, about 200 miles from its source near Mount Hermon, through the Sea of Galilee to the Dead Sea. East of the River Jordan were the lands of Bashan, Gilead, Ammon and Moab.

The land of Canaan, therefore, lay between the great Middle Eastern centres of civilization, and it was a natural corridor for both traders and invading armies. If the successive governments of Egypt or Mesopotamia pursued expansionist policies, or waged war on each other, Canaan was all too likely to become embroiled in the conflict. In addition, its diverse geographical features and the mixed ethnic origins of its inhabitants led to difficulties in forming a single political entity. The Jews themselves believe that their ancestor Abraham was an immigrant and came to Canaan as a 'wandering Aramaean' (Deuteronomy 26:5). They maintain that their crucial religious experience occurred outside the country, when they were crossing the Sinai wilderness. Since they settled in Canaan, they have never been the sole possessors of the territory, yet the land remains central to their understanding of themselves. To this day the promise to

Abraham reverberates in the Jewish community: 'Lift up your eyes and look from the place where you are, northward and southward and eastward and westward. For all the land which you see I will give to you and to your descendants for ever' (Genesis 13:14, 15).

2. ARCHAEOLOGY OF THE ANCIENT MIDDLE EAST

Much of what we know about the beliefs and practices of the inhabitants of the ancient Middle East of this period is derived from archaeological excavation. Ruins of ancient fortified cities from the third millennium BCE have been found along the length of the Eastern Mediterranean coast. Particularly significant are the remains found at Tel Mardikh in Syria, the ancient city of Ebla, where an immense archive of tablets has been discovered. They are inscribed in a western Semitic language and, besides giving detailed records of the city's administration and diplomacy, they contain names similar to those found in the biblical accounts of the Patriarchs Abraham, Isaac and Jacob. However, it must be emphasized that these tablets reflect a situation prevalent at least 400 years before the time of the Patriarchs themselves.

The incursions of the Amurru or Amorites are evident at such sites as Ras Shamra-Ugarit, Megiddo, Byblos, Jericho and Lachish. In Jericho, for example, the wall of the city was completely burnt in c. 2300 BCE and the town seems to have been virtually uninhabited for a period. The same gap is found in Ras Shamra-Ugarit and Lachish, and the area of devastation stretches from Mesopotamia in the east to Byblos on the coast. It seems to have lasted until early in the twentieth century BCE, when there are signs of recovery.

It is possible that the biblical records of the Patriarchs reflect memories of this later period; if so, Abraham and his descendants must be identified with Amorite nomads who wandered throughout the land of Canaan, south into Egypt and east through Mesopotamia. While following their herds from place to place, they would have been aware of the increased security of the urban centres round which they travelled. Excavations at Mari, for example, show a highly successful civilization. In the late eighteenth century BCE, the King of Mari lived in an extensive palace with 300 rooms, and a huge library of tablets has been discovered there, including legal and economic documents. The names of some of Abraham's kinsfolk correspond to the names of some of the towns recorded in the texts, and the frequent attacks of passing nomadic tribes are also mentioned. Ultimately, Mari was destroyed by King Hammurabi of Babylon.

Texts have also been discovered to the east of the Tigris river at Nuzu, dating back to the fifteenth century BCE and giving us a vivid picture of town life. Particularly interesting for the student of Jewish history are the customs they describe, which echo incidents in the stories of the Patriarchs. Examples include the provision by a barren wife of a concubine for her husband (see Genesis 16) and the fact that possession of the household gods gave inheritance rights (Genesis 31). Yet it is important not to make too much of these connections. The texts have to be viewed very selectively, and many of the practices at Nuzu have no counterparts in the biblical accounts.

Palace archives have also been found at Ras Shamra-Ugarit. This library dates from the fifteenth to fourteenth centuries BCE and is associated with the excavated temples of Baal and Dagon (pagan gods also mentioned in the Bible). The documents include the texts of Canaanite religious myths; we know a little of the Canaanite religion from the tirades of the biblical prophets against it. The Ras Shamra tablets indicate that it was basically a fertility cult with many gods and goddesses personifying the powers of the natural world. It was the religion of a settled and agricultural people and as such was tempting to a nomadic tribe such as the Israelites when they were trying to adjust to a different way of life after the conquest. The Bible makes it clear that their uncompromising desert god JHWH was a very different character from the anthropomorphic Canaanite deities.

Finally, tablets dating from the early fourteenth century have been found at Tell el-Amarna. These are letters from Canaanite and Syrian kings to their Egyptian overlord, and in particular they complain of the activities of the 'Apira', who were creating disturbances in the area.

3. LAW IN MESOPOTAMIA AND BABYLON

There have been attempts to date the Patriarchs by identifying the King Hammurabi who destroyed Mari with Amraphel, one of the four kings against whom Abraham fought in Genesis 14. This, of course, is nonsense; a tribal chief such as Abraham could never have defeated a king of imperial Babylon. A more interesting connection is with the legal codes and treaties of Babylon and Mesopotamia, which have definite similarities to the laws and customs of the Jewish people.

The oldest collection of laws so far discovered dates from 2050 BCE and is known as the Sumerian Code. It was drawn up by Ur Nammu, who describes himself as 'King of Sumer and Akkad' and whose capital was Ur in southern Mesopotamia. According to Genesis 11:28, Ur was also Abraham's native city. Ur Nammu's code describes how the god Nanna chose the king to rule the land as his representative. The king fulfilled his obligations by removing dishonest officials from their positions, by establishing a system of weights and measures and by introducing set fines for those who victimized the poor and the oppressed. The same preoccupation with justice and with fair weights and measures is to be found in Leviticus 19: 35–36: 'You shall do no wrong in judgment, in measures of length of weight or quantity . . . I am the Lord your God who brought you out of the Land of Egypt.'

Another collection has been found near Baghdad and relates to the ancient kingdom of Eshunna. Again the god (in this case Tishpak) has delegated his authority to the king. The laws are written in Akkadian on two tablets and probably date from c. 1920 BCE. They mainly relate to property and include one provision that reads: 'If an ox is known to gore habitually and it gores a man to death, then the owner of the ox shall pay two-thirds of a mina of silver.' Provisions for the victims of a violent ox are also to be found in Exodus 21:21–32.

Another Sumerian code was drawn up by King Lipit Ishtar in the Kingdom of Isin in the early nineteenth century BCE, and it has similarities to the earlier code of Ur Nammu. More complete is the code of Hammurabi of Babylon, who ruled between 1728 and 1686 BCE. One version of the code, inscribed in Akkadian on a six-foot-high black tablet, was discovered in Susa. Again it begins by claiming that the king's authority was given by the god (this time Marduk), then follow almost 300 provisions covering social, commercial, moral and domestic life. Some of the provisions echo those of the earlier codes and they are mainly arranged according to a set formula – 'If a man does . . . then . . .'. The code concludes with an epilogue expressing the king's hope that justice will be maintained and that the oppressed will receive their rightful due, because 'Hammurabi, the lord, who is like a real father to his people, bestirred himself for the word of Marduk his Lord . . . '

The oldest corpus of Jewish law is found in what is called the Book of the Covenant (Exodus 20:22–23:33). Like the Babylonian and Mesopotamian codes, it evokes divine authority: 'The Lord said to Moses, "Thus you shall say to the people of Israel, 'You have seen for yourselves that I have talked with you from Heaven' . . . " ' Many of the subsequent provisions follow the same formula, as in, 'If a man seduce a virgin who is not betrothed and lies with her, he will give the marriage present for her and make her his wife' (Exodus 22:16), and the code also ends with an epilogue. This is not to say that the Israelite code is identical to or even based on the code of Hammurabi, but there are clear parallels in both form and content.

Another similarity has been found between the formulations of Israelite law and those of Hittite and Assyrian treaties between king and vassal. These treaties date back as early as the second millennium BCE, and include a prologue describing the benevolence of the ruler, the rules which the vassal must accept, the deposition of the treaty in a sanctuary, the regular recitation of the provisions of the treaty and a list of the rewards and punishments entailed if the treaty is honoured or broken. Again we find parallels with the covenants made between God and the Israelites as recorded in the Pentateuch. There is no doubt that the laws of Israel were written later than the Mesopotamian codes and treaties, but nonetheless there is clear evidence that they emerged from a common background.

4. ANCIENT MIDDLE EASTERN RELIGION

Also from archaeological excavations, we know a great deal about the religions of the ancient Mesopotamians, Egyptians, Hittites and Canaanites. King Ashurbanipal of Assyria, who ruled from 668 to 633 BCE, amassed a huge collection of translated texts, many of which may have been originally composed early in the second millennium. From these tablets, we learn that the peoples of Mesopotamia recorded their version of the Creation story and they also preserved myths of death and resurrection and a great flood. The Creation was seen as the result of a primeval conflict between Apsu and Tiamat, the gods of water, and the divine hero, Marduk, who formed Heaven and Earth from the corpses of his opponents. Human beings were created to be the servants of the gods and the city of Babylon was built as Marduk's residence. Death and resurrection was the theme of the myth of Tammuz and Ishtar. Tammuz, the god of vegetation, died, was imprisoned in the underworld and was rescued by Ishtar, the Queen of Heaven. The Mesopotamian story of the flood involved a deluge sent by the gods to destroy humanity, and the rescue of the pious Utnapishtun in a huge boat. There are many modifications of these three myths, including the famous Epic of Gilgamesh, dated in the Akkadian version from the seventh century BCE, but based on a far earlier Sumerian account.

Egyptian mythology is a vast, complicated subject. Unlike the Sumerian and Babylonian kings, who, as we have seen, saw themselves as the representatives of the gods, the Egyptian king believed himself to be the god incarnate. During his lifetime he was Horus, the son of Osiris and his sister Isis, but after death he became Osiris. The Osiris–Horus cult produced many myths. Like Tammuz, Osiris was the god of vegetation who underwent death and resurrection, and he was also king of the underworld. Another important figure was Re or Atum, the sun god, who had a secret name of power and was prominent in Egyptian Creation myths. Like Osiris, Re was associated with kingship, and later there seems to have been a fusion between the cults of the two gods.

We know of the Hittite religion from the tablets excavated at Boghaz-Koi. The Hittites, who are mentioned in the biblical list of peoples inhabiting the land of Canaan before the Israelite invasion, built an extensive empire in Asia Minor that lasted from c. 2000 until 1200 BCE. Many of their myths seem to have been similar to those of Mesopotamia, and they have a strong folklore element. The gods and goddesses feuded among themselves; the younger generation defied the older, and their battles involved the destruction of a great dragon by the storm god and the death and resurrection of the fertility god.

The discovery of the Ras Shamra tablets at Ugarit in 1928 has added enormously to our knowledge of the ancient people of Canaan. The tablets were written in an ancient Semitic language and their religious material falls into three main groups: the adventures of the god Baal, the story of Keret, King of Hubur, and the legend of King Aqhat. Baal was a fertility god and the son of the high god, El (sometimes called Bull-El). He was described as the 'rider of the clouds', who sent lightning and thunder as well as life-giving rain. He slaughtered the dragon Lotan, who represents the forces of chaos, and overcame the fearsome river god, Yam-Nahar. Subsequently he was captured by Mot, the king of the underworld, then was rescued by his sister, Anath, and finally the two achieved some sort of reconciliation. The story of Keret tells how the king failed to fulfil a vow to the goddess Asherah, was punished and was ultimately forgiven by El, the father of the gods. King Aqhat was killed by Anath because she wanted his bow and as a result there was famine in the land for seven years; it seems likely that the story would end with Aqhat's resurrection, but the final tablets are lost.

This, then, was the religious milieu in which the ancestors of the Jewish people found themselves. The biblical writers were well aware of the seductiveness of the pagan world view, and again and again in the Bible we find injunctions to have nothing whatever to do with the indigenous people of the land of Canaan. Nonetheless, despite themselves, the Israelites were influenced by the ideas of the neighbouring peoples when they established their own patterns of belief and worship.

5. THE EMERGENCE OF THE JEWS

As we have seen, the Jews believe themselves to be descended from the Patriarch Abraham. According to the account in the book of Genesis, Abraham was a native of the Mesopotamian city of Ur, who lived for a time in Haran and then wandered with his flocks and herds throughout the land of Canaan. God promised that he would be the father of a great nation and, as a symbol of the promise, the practice of circumcision was instituted (Genesis 17): 'Every male among you shall be circumcised . . . It will be a sign of the covenant between me and you . . . He that is eight days old among you shall be circumcised.' To this day all Jewish boys are circumcised on their eighth day of life.

Jews trace their descent through Abraham's son Isaac and through Isaac's son Jacob (also called Israel). Jacob settled with his twelve sons in the land of Egypt, where their descendants were subsequently made slaves. Several generations later, according to the book of Exodus, these twelve tribes of Israelites were liberated from their enslavement under the leadership of Moses and, after further wanderings, took possession of the Promised Land of Canaan.

This understanding of the early history of the Jewish people was enshrined in the liturgy. According to the Deuteronomy 26:5–9, every Jew must present the first fruits of his produce to God and, as he does so, recite the following formula: 'A wandering Aramaean was my father and he went down into Egypt and sojourned there, few in number; and there he became a nation, great, mighty and populous. And the Egyptians treated us harshly and afflicted us and laid upon us hard bondage. Then we cried to the Lord, the God of our fathers, and the Lord brought us out of Egypt with a mighty hand and an outstretched arm, with great terror, with signs and wonders; and He brought us into this place and gave us this land, a land flowing with milk and honey.'

We cannot assess the accuracy of this folk memory. It is certainly possible that the patriarchal wanderings were part of the general movement of the Amurru or Amorites away from the cities in the nineteenth and eighteenth centuries BCE. Some scholars maintain that Abraham, Isaac and Jacob were individual historical people, while others (perhaps encouraged by the evidence of the Mari tablets) argue that their names refer to places or to tribes. A particularly intractable problem is that of the relationship of the ancestors of the Jews with a group known as the 'Apiru.

The 'Apiru are first mentioned in the documents of the eighteenth century BCE; where they appear as bands of warriors. The Mari texts mention the 'Apiru contributing to the general confusion of the time. The names of 'Apiru individuals indicate that they were of mixed ethnic origin, but they seem to have shared a common inferior status, and occasionally it is noted that they were fugitives, strangers or refugees. It would be tempting simply to identify these 'Apiru with early Hebrews, but this is improbable, since the 'Apiru were a social rather than an ethnic group. The Patriarchs may have been part of the 'Apiru element in Canaan, but the two groups were certainly not identical.

There have also been scholarly attempts to place the biblical emigration to Egypt in the period of the seventeenth and sixteenth centuries. At that time Egypt was ruled by an Asiatic dynasty, the Hyksos; these kings, it is argued, would have been welcoming to Semitic newcomers such as Jacob and his sons and would have given them high positions. Then, when the book of Exodus declares that there arose a king 'who did not know Joseph', this refers to the subsequent non-Hyksos ruler who wished to purge the kingdom of Asiatic elements. Again this is a tidy solution, but Asiatic nomads entered Egypt for trade purposes or as prisoners of war throughout the second millennium, and the dates of the Exodus and the conquest of the Promised Land are not so easy to determine. A probable solution is that many Asiatic groups went down to Egypt, and most of the tribes who eventually colonized Canaan may have been descended from some of them. There is also evidence that some of the Israelite tribes had no tradition of a sojourn in Egypt and this group may have remained as nomads in the area throughout the period. It is certainly possible that both groups may have had some connection with the marauding bands of 'Apiru mentioned in the Tell el-Amarna texts, and it was this recognition of a common heritage that enabled the immigrating tribes to be assimilated.

SUGGESTED FURTHER READING

Encyclopaedia Judaica, 'Habiru', Keter, 1972.
S. H. Hooke, *Middle Eastern Mythology*, Penguin, 1963.
Kathleen M. Kenyon, *The Bible and Recent Archaeology*, Colonnade, 1978.
T. L. Thompson, *The Historicity of the Patriarchal Narratives*, de Gruyter, 1974.

2 THE PENTATEUCH

1. THE STATUS OF THE PENTATEUCH IN JEWISH THEOLOGY

The first five books of the Bible, Genesis, Exodus, Leviticus, Numbers and Deuteronomy, are known collectively as the Torah (Hebrew 'Teaching'). The Jews call their Bible the Tanakh, which is an acronym of Torah (the Pentateuch), Nevi'im (Prophets) and Ketuvim (Writings or Hagiography). Torah, in its most general sense, means 'law', and Torah can refer to all Jewish law, both written and oral. The written law is found in the Pentateuch – hence the use of the term Torah to mean the first five books of the Bible.

The Pentateuch is our main source of information about the early history of the Jewish people. As we have seen in the last chapter, archaeological evidence from the ancient Middle East has, to some extent, confirmed the background to the laws and customs recorded in the Bible. Nonetheless our knowledge of the history of the Patriarchs, the exodus from Egypt and the organization of the twelve tribes comes entirely from the Pentateuch, and therefore we must ask whether it is a reliable account.

The traditional Jewish view is that the Torah was given to Moses on Mount Sinai by God. According to the Numbers 12:6–8, God declared: 'If there is a prophet among you, I, the Lord, make myself known to him in a vision; I speak to him in a dream. Not so with my servant Moses; he is entrusted with all my house. With him I speak mouth to mouth clearly and not in dark speech; and he beholds the form of the Lord.' In Exodus

33:11, Moses is said to have spoken with God 'face to face as a man speaks to his friend'. Thus the revelation to Moses is believed to be unique and, to an Orthodox Jew, the question of its reliability is absurd. It was given directly by God and therefore must be true in every particular.

This conviction was expressed very clearly by the mediaeval philosopher Maimonides. He formulated the Thirteen Principles of the Jewish Faith, the eighth of which maintains that the Torah we have in our possession is the same as that which was given to Moses and is of divine origin. In handing down the Torah, Moses was like a scribe writing from dictation, and Orthodox Judaism rejects any form of literary or textual criticism. The Pentateuch has been copied and recopied down the ages with minute attention to detail because it is believed to be literally the word of God.

The Torah Scrolls are the most sacred object in a synagogue. They are made of parchment and the text is written by hand; it is rolled on two wooden staves, known as the 'azei hayyim' (trees of life), and the whole is bound with a decorated wrapper. It is then 'dressed' in a mantle of some rich material or kept in a leather or metal case. The staves are decorated with finials which are encased in a crown. Over the dressed scroll is hung a breastplate, reminiscent of the breastplate of the High Priest. A pointer ('yad') is used to aid reading, because the scroll itself may not be touched. It is kept in the Ark of the synagogue, which is the focal point of the building. When the Ark is opened the congregation stands up in recognition of their respect and devotion to the scrolls within.

The Pentateuch itself is divided into fifty-four portions. One is read every Sabbath so that the whole can be completed in the course of a year. The cycle begins on the Sabbath after Sukkot (the festival of tabernacles) and is completed on the final day of that festival, known as Simhat Torah (the rejoicing in the law). When the scroll is taken from the Ark, it is carried in procession around the synagogue. Then different men from the congregation are summoned in turn to read part of the week's portion, beginning and ending with a benediction. The Torah can only be read if at least ten adult men are present (a 'minyan') and the reading forms the central part of the service. When the portion is finished, the scroll is held up and displayed to the congregation, who declare: 'This is the Law which Moses set before the Children of Israel, according to the commandment of the Lord by the hand of Moses. It is a tree of life to them that grasp it, and of them that uphold it, everyone is rendered happy.'

Thus Orthodox Jews regard the Pentateuch as God's ultimate revelation to His people. It is crowned like a king and decorated like the high priest, and its precepts must be followed for no other reason than that they are instructions from God Himself. Its chronicle of events must be accurate in every respect because God is the author.

2. THE AUTHORSHIP OF THE PENTATEUCH

Modern scholarly investigation has called into question the traditional Orthodox view of the Pentateuch. As early as the sixteenth century, it was conjectured that the first five books of the Bible were compiled from different sources. Stories seem to be repeated, and there are notable stylistic differences within the text. The first chapter of the story of Joseph (Genesis 37) illustrates this very clearly. Joseph's father is called both Jacob and Israel; the brothers hate Joseph because of his dreams and because his father favours him by giving him a special coat; Reuben tries to save Joseph, but so also does Judah, and Joseph appears to be sold to both Ishmaelite and Midianite traders. These discrepancies can only be explained if the final account was derived from more than one source.

Other factors also call into question the authorship of Moses. The text contains anachronisms, such as Genesis 36:31–39, which is a list of the kings of Edom. These are said to rule 'before there were any kings in Israel'. But there were no kings in Israel until many centuries after the death of Moses. Another factor is the duplication of actual stories; both Beersheba and Bethel are given their names twice (Genesis 21:1 and 26:33, and Genesis 28:19 and 35:15) and both Abraham and Isaac try to pass off their wives as their sisters to protect themselves (Genesis 12 and 26:1–11). There are also inconsistencies: in Genesis 1, human beings are created after all the other animals, but in Genesis 2, man at any rate is made before the other creatures. The laws set out in the book of Deuteronomy are slightly different from those in the rest of the Pentateuch – for example, Exodus 22:24 allows sacrifice to be offered in 'every place that I set aside for you to worship me', while Deuteronomy 12:14 insists that it can only be offered in the 'one place the Lord will choose'. Perhaps most significantly, God is called by different names. Exodus 6 insists that Moses is the first to call God by his proper name JHWH, but, according to Genesis 4:26, men began to call on the name of JHWH from the time of the first man Adam's grandchildren. In addition there are many other passages in which He is not referred to as JHWH (normally translated as 'the Lord'), but as Elohim ('God'), and JHWH and Elohim reveal themselves to humanity in rather different ways.

In the middle of the nineteenth century, two German scholars, Karl Heinrich Graf and Julius Wellhausen, concluded that these discrepancies could only be explained if it was accepted that the five books of Moses were compiled from four different sources that once existed separately. The first document, which they called J because it referred to God as JHWH, originated in the Southern Kingdom of Judah in the ninth century BCE. The second document, known as E because God was called Elohim, stemmed from the Northern Kingdom in the eighth century. Later J and E were combined into one. The D source, which was mainly found in the book of Deuteronomy, was composed in the seventh century, and the P source, which was primarily concerned with priestly matters and the sacrificial cult, went back to the sixth century. Although the sources preserved many ancient traditions, inevitably they also reflected the preoccupations of their compilers.

Since the time of Graf and Wellhausen, this hypothesis has been considerably modified. Some scholars are unhappy with the idea of written sources and prefer to speak of 'circles of tradition'. J, E, P and D are seen not as documents, as was originally suggested, but as different oral traditions that circulated among different groups. Some of these traditions may go back much farther than the dates given by Graf and Wellhausen, but they were modified and updated as the tales were retold. Other scholars reject the idea of separate definable sources altogether, and maintain that the text of the Pentateuch was finally compiled from a multitude of oral traditions. In any event, among scholars who have no religious presuppositions, there is a general recognition that the first five books of the Bible were not written by Moses and that they are rather a collection of traditions originating at different times. As we have seen in the previous chapter, there are strong parallels in the text with the laws, customs and myths of the other ancient Middle Eastern civilizations. It does seem therefore as if the Pentateuch grew out of a specific cultural context. It is not, so to speak, 'created out of nothing'.

3. THE JE SOURCES

Although the precise boundaries of the different sources of the Pentateuch are still much disputed by scholars, it will be helpful in our tracing of the early history of the Jewish people if we follow the lines suggested by the supporters of the Graf–Wellhausen thesis. J, the earliest source, is a compilation of early folklore and religious history, the whole inspired by a particular theological viewpoint. Primarily the aim of the writer seems to have been to show God's constant interest and involvement in the affairs of His chosen people.

The narrative begins with the story of Adam and Eve, the first human beings. Despite being given every blessing, they listen to the serpent (much in evidence in the Canaanite fertility cults) and are disobedient to their Creator. In consequence they are expelled from Eden and have to confront the problems and difficulties of the outside world. The first disaster is the murder of one of their sons by the other. Cain, who represents the settled Canaanite way of life, kills the nomadic shepherd Abel. This is followed by the tale of the great flood. Humanity, in the shape of Noah and his family, is given another chance, but even Noah is seduced by the relative ease of agriculture. He plants a vineyard; he becomes drunk; his son Ham sees him naked and intoxicated and, as forefather of the Canaanites, he is cursed and is condemned to be a slave to his brothers. Finally, after the tale of the Tower of Babel in which, again, humanity is punished for its hubris, we come to the stories of the Patriarch Abraham.

The J source covers many of Abraham's travels and includes the sagas of Lot and the doomed cities of Sodom and Gomorrah. However, the emphasis is on the covenant and the blessing of the Jewish people. God tells Abraham that He will make him the father of a great nation and that all the land he sees will be given to his descendants forever. Miraculously the elderly Sarah, Abraham's wife, has a child, Isaac, who is the inheritor of the promise. Originally the Isaac stories almost certainly circulated separately from the Abraham cycle. Again there is rivalry between two brothers, this time between Isaac's twin sons, Esau and Jacob. The younger brother Jacob defeats the older (again a settled farmer) and is given a new name, Israel. In his turn, he is the father of twelve sons, the ancestors of the twelve tribes of Israel. Then follows the long story of Joseph in which the J source is skilfully interwoven with the E. It explains how the inheritors of the covenant with Abraham, the descendants of the Patriarch Jacob, find themselves in Egypt, how God looks after His chosen ones and how, with God's help, evil can be transformed into good.

The story of the exodus from Egypt, like the saga of Joseph, is a mixture of both the J and the E sources. J seems to have understood the event as a flight rather than as an expulsion, and it is followed by the account of Moses' tremendous encounter with God on Mount Sinai. Moses is portrayed as the central figure of the story and many scholars attribute the 'ritual version' of the Ten Commandments (Exodus 34:14–26) to the J editor. Historically speaking it is unlikely that all the tribes who eventually settled in the Promised Land were descended from the rabble of slaves that Moses led up from Egypt, but due to the skill of the J compiler, we certainly receive the impression that they were the crucial group.

The E editor, working in the Northern Kingdom about a century later, seems to have believed that God's real name, JHWH, was only revealed in the time of Moses, in contrast to the J source, which maintains that it was known to the earliest human beings. E is less interested in primeval history. In his stories of the Patriarchs, he tells us of the horrifying episode of God's command to Abraham to sacrifice his beloved son Isaac. Isaac was the inheritor of the promise, but without hesitation Abraham prepared to obey God's will. He provides an extraordinary model of submission and faith, and he is rewarded by a renewal of the promise. God also providentially delivers His people (this time from the hands of the Egyptians) after the expulsion from Egypt. Moses is portrayed as the great mediator between God and humanity, but he is unique; for E the distance between God and His people is immense. In general God does not make direct contact with individuals, but instead conveys His wishes through angels or by dreams or prophecy. God is a supremely righteous God. According to the E source, He makes His commandments known, and history is perceived primarily as the arena in which the Jewish people display either their faithfulness or their disobedience to the divine will.

4. THE D SOURCE

The book of Deuteronomy has a very different character from the books of Genesis, Exodus, Leviticus, and Numbers, and is in many ways closer to the historical books of Joshua, Judges, Samuel and Kings. It falls into three parts. First the main events of the Israelites' journey from Horeb (the Deuteronomic name for Sinai) to the land of Moab are described; secondly God's law, as given on Horeb, is explained and expounded, and thirdly the Jewish people are presented with the choice of obedience or disobedience. Despite the fact that the book is so different from the rest of the Pentateuch and that it ends with an account of the death of Moses, its Mosaic authorship remains an article of faith for Orthodox Jews. This, of course, is what gives it its authority in the Jewish community even today.

Most scholars, however, believe that the core of Deuteronomy is associated with the law book found in the Temple of Jerusalem in the reign of King Josiah. According to the second book of Kings, when the book was discovered Josiah was so impressed with its contents that he began a radical programme of religious reform that involved the centralization of all religious worship in Jerusalem. The book itself is described as a 'Covenant document' and it takes a similar form to contemporary Hittite and Assyrian treaties between kings and vassals (see Chapter 1, Part 3). It contains the usual prologue, the general principles to be obeyed, the detailed obligations, the deposition of the agreement in the sanctuary, arrangements for the regular recitation of the document and a list of rewards and punishments. The writer of Deuteronomy believed that the key to the Jewish people's existence lay in obedience to God's commandments. As he put it, 'See I have set before you this day life and good, death and evil. If you obey the commandments of the Lord your God . . . then you shall live and multiply. But if your heart turns away . . . I declare to you this day that you shall perish' (30:15–18).

What then are the laws that the Jewish people must keep if they are to survive? First and foremost the Jews must remain faithful to God. They must not be tempted by the religion of the Canaanites, which they encountered once they had settled in the Promised Land. It was JHWH, the Lord, who had revealed Himself in history, who had liberated them from bondage in the land of Egypt, who had given them His immutable law through Moses on Mount Sinai and who had led them through the wilderness to Canaan. Even though they might discard the nomadic way of life associated with the Patriarchs and Moses and might become settled farmers like the Canaanites, there was no justification for abandoning the one God who had chosen them from among all the nations of the earth.

In fact, the Deuteronomic laws cover a multitude of subjects. Although their first concern is the maintenance of the covenant relationship with God, many laws also deal with the correct attitude to the weak and the oppressed in society. Such regulations as forgiving debts every seven years (Chapter 15), the responsible conduct of warfare (Chapter 20), the fair treatment of children (Chapter 21) and the laws of usury (Chapter 23) all reflect a real humanitarian concern. God is understood as the God of the weak and humble as well as of the powerful and strong. The Jewish people are reminded that they themselves were once slaves and it was JHWH who rescued and delivered them. In remembrance the Israelites are not to treat their hired servants harshly; they must not swindle the fatherless; they must leave some of their crops for the widow and the destitute and even the ox may not be muzzled when he treads out the grain (Chapters 24 and 25).

Finally, the writer of Deuteronomy is emphatic that sacrifice to God may only be performed at one central sanctuary. The small hill altars associated with Canaanite practices must be pulled down. Three times a year, on the pilgrim festivals of Pesah (Passover), Shavuot (Weeks) and Sukkot (Tabernacles), all adult males must present themselves at the central place of worship and no other sanctuary may be substituted. Since the laws of Deuteronomy were supposed to have been laid down by Moses, it could not be specified that the one sanctuary was in Jerusalem; Jerusalem was only conquered by the Israelites several centuries after Moses' death. Nonetheless, if we accept that the core of Deuteronomy was composed in the seventh century bce, by that stage everyone knew exactly which sanctuary was meant: sacrifice was only legitimate in Jerusalem. This prohibition had an enormous and unexpected effect on the history and religion of the Jewish people once the Jerusalem Temple was finally destroyed.

5. THE P SOURCE

The P source is thought to date from the sixth century BCE. Like J and E, P cannot be traced to a definite document, but its strand is easily recognized in the books of Genesis, Exodus, Leviticus and Numbers. The style is distinctive, with an emphasis on lists and measurements, and it is frequently repetitious and poetic. The writer shows a particular interest in the religious ritual of the Israelites and is known as P because he is thought to have come from a priestly background. The Holiness Code of Leviticus (Chapters 17–26) in particular is ascribed to him, and the historical events he describes in Genesis and Exodus emphasize the sacred nature of Israel's history.

The poetic account of the Creation of the world in seven days (Genesis 1) is thought to be his composition. God separated light from darkness, created the world's atmosphere, divided the seas from the dry land and caused vegetation to grow. He formed the sun, moon and stars and created times and seasons; He made the sea creatures and birds and finally formed the land creatures and human beings. Then on the seventh day He rested, thus giving the world the weekly Sabbath. In some ways the account is similar to that of the Mesopotamian Creation epics (see Chapter 1, Part 4), but unlike Marduk, who destroys the powers of the chaotic Tiamat, the God of the priestly writer stands completely outside the natural world. He does not, as in the JE source, walk in the garden in the cool of the day and converse with the creatures He has made. He is outside the world and He sees that it is good.

It is in the P source that the covenant with Noah is described. After the flood, God sends a rainbow and promises that He will never again try to destroy His creatures with a flood. He announces the beginning of a system of law and order and indicates that there will be penalties for crime. Noah and his family are to be the ancestors of all humanity, but it is the descendants of Abraham who will be the agents of the world's final salvation. God says to the Patriarch, 'By your descendants shall all the nations of the world bless themselves because you have obeyed my voice' (Genesis 22:18). The priestly writer gives his own version of the covenant with Abraham, and the ritual of circumcision is explained (see Chapter 1, Part 5).

According to the P source Aaron, the brother of Moses, is the first High Priest. He is also appointed to be the guardian of the law, because the Jewish people are chosen to be a holy people. The God who brought them out of the Land of Egypt is a holy God and, as His people, they too must be holy. Among many other things, holiness involves only eating meat from particular kinds of animals, birds, or fish. For an animal to be clean it must both chew the cud and have a cloven hoof; cows and sheep fall into that category, while rabbits and pigs do not. Fish must have both fins and scales, like herring or mackerel – all shellfish are forbidden. Carrion birds must also be rejected. The blood of any creature may not be consumed, and there is the mysterious prohibition that kids may not be boiled in their mothers' milk. Over the centuries these rules have been discussed and interpreted, and the whole elaborate system of Kashrut ('clean food') has been devised. But it should be stressed that Jews have observed these laws not for reasons of hygiene or for any practical advantage, but because they believe themselves to be a holy people who must be totally obedient to the commandments of God.

It is also to the priestly code that the extensive laws for Yom Kippur (the Day of Atonement) belong. Once a year, Aaron as High Priest is instructed to sacrifice a goat for the people as a sin offering. Another goat should also be presented to God; Aaron must confess the sins of the people over it and then release it into the wilderness. It will carry all their iniquities away. The Day of Atonement, which is to be a Sabbath of solemn rest, provides a mechanism by which the sins of the Jewish people can be forgiven and they can in consequence retain their status as a people holy to the Lord.

The priestly source was almost certainly composed during the exile in Babylon (see Chapter 3, Part 5). The account of the earliest days and the writer's understanding of the role of the Jewish people among the nations enabled the Israelites to survive the catastrophe of the first destruction of the Jerusalem Temple in 586 BCE. No longer were they merely a political entity clinging to their Promised Land; rather they had become a worshipping community centred round a sacrificial cult and an elaborate system of ritual and moral laws. Although their God was the God of all humanity, it was their little group that would lead the world in its spiritual quest.

SUGGESTED FURTHER READING

D.J.A. Clines, *The Theme of the Pentateuch*, JSOT, 1978.
Louis Jacobs, *We Have Reason to Believe*, Vallentine Mitchell, 1957.
G. von Rad, *The Problem of the Hexateuch and Other Essays*, Oliver and Boyd, 1966.
J. Wellhausen, *Prolegomena to the History of Israel*, A. and C. Black, 1885.

3 FROM CONQUEST TO EXILE

1. CONQUEST AND SETTLEMENT

The story of the conquest and settlement of the Promised Land is told in the books of Joshua and Judges. According to Deuteronomy, Moses died before reaching Canaan and Joshua became the next Israelite leader.

The exact date of the conquest is uncertain – some scholars favour the thirteenth and some the fifteenth century BCE. Certainly the archaeological evidence is inconclusive. The biblical account maintains that the Israelites took the city of Jericho and the walls fell down; excavations at the site of Jericho do show signs of the walls having been destroyed by fire, but unfortunately at a much earlier date. At other sites there is evidence of destruction in the Canaanite cities of the thirteenth century, and a sophisticated culture seems to have been replaced by something more primitive. However, we do not know whether Israelite culture was less sophisticated than Canaanite and, in any case, the cities that seem to have been destroyed are not identical with the cities mentioned in the book of Joshua. The remains of Ai, for example, which is said to have been burnt to the ground (Joshua 8) shows no signs of such destruction.

From Egyptian records we know that the land of Canaan had been under Egyptian control for most of the second millennium. Each city was independent, but owed allegiance to the Egyptian king. Inland, life was less regulated and there was a shifting nomadic population. By the thirteenth century the grip of Egypt was loosening; the Philistines, originally from Crete, had moved in and had established themselves in their own city states in Ashdod, Ashkelon, Ekron, Gath and Gaza. As we have seen, there were changes in the other Canaanite cities. The first reference to Israel outside the Bible is found on an Egyptian stone monument and dates from c. 1220; King Meneptah of Egypt is said to have 'laid waste Israel'.

The book of Joshua gives the impression that the Israelites, with God on their side, won an impressive array of battles and that the Promised Land became theirs almost immediately. Some scholars believe this to be an exaggeration, and think that the conquest was more like an infiltration. The Israelites settled in the less-controlled hill country and gradually became the dominant element in the population, subsequently being able to take over the cities. Yet another theory is that certain of the twelve tribes had never gone down into Egypt, that they were already established in Canaan and, recognizing their affinity with the nomadic Exodus tribes, they encouraged their settlement. The history of the conquest is clearly complex and problematic – despite the successes reported in the book of Joshua, the book of Judges gives a rather different picture.

The judges seem to have been charismatic leaders who arose when the people were threatened by external enemies. Deborah fought against the Canaanites, Ehud the Moabites, Gideon the Midianites, Jephthah the Ammonites and Samson the Philistines. The Israelites were clearly not in complete control. The Song of Deborah (Judges 5), which may well date back to the twelfth century BCE, indicates that Deborah and her general Barak managed to unite six of the Israelite tribes in the face of a common foe. On another occasion the eleven tribes united to punish the Benjaminites (Judges 20). It has been suggested that the Israelites' association at this time was similar to that of a Greek amphictyony; they were bound together by their allegiance to one God and to a shared system of worship. The Ark of the Covenant, which had been built in the wilderness and contained the tablets of the law, was kept at a central shrine (Shechem, Mizpah, Gilgal, Bethel and Shiloh are all mentioned). There the Israelites gathered regularly to be reminded of their history and of their obligations under the covenant.

In the early days there seems to have been a strong feeling against having a monarchical system of government. The Canaanites had kings, but the judge Gideon declares, 'I will not rule over you and my son will not rule over you. The Lord will rule over you' (Judges 8:23). As the Psalmist put it many years later, 'The Lord is King for ever and ever'

(Psalm 10:16). Nonetheless, by the eleventh century it had become clear that the Philistines in particular were a real threat to the Jewish people. The tribes needed to unite against them on a more permanent basis – a charismatic judge was not going to be enough.

2. THE UNITED MONARCHY

According to I Samuel 11, a young man called Saul rallied the twelve tribes against the Ammonites and in consequence was acclaimed king. The text indicates that this was not a step that was taken lightly; on the one hand the Israelites needed a strong and permanent leader, but on the other the anointing of a king would undermine God's role as the only ruler of His people.

Ultimately Saul emerges from the biblical account as a tragic figure. Despite being supported initially by the last judge, Samuel, he made little headway against the Philistines, and as time went on Samuel turned away from him. Saul became increasingly suspicious of one of his young warriors, David, and finally died by his own hand after a terrible defeat by the Philistines on Mount Gilboa. David's lament over the bodies of Saul and his son Jonathan is one of the greatest lyrics of literature:

> Saul and Jonathan, beloved and lovely!
> In life and in death they were not divided.
> They were swifter than eagles.
> They were stronger than lions. . . .
> How are the mighty fallen and the weapons of war perished.
> (II Samuel 1:19–27)

David, on the other hand, is portrayed as one of the great heroes of Israel and tales of his military exploits (such as the killing of Goliath) have become part of the folklore of western civilization. After Saul's death he was immediately anointed king by the two southern tribes, Judah and Benjamin, which had always been slightly separated from the northern tribes. For seven years David was king of the Southern Kingdom. Saul's son, Ishbosheth, had become king of the northern tribes, but he enjoyed little popular support and once the commander-in-chief of his army defected to David, David became ruler of the whole kingdom and the twelve tribes were once more united.

The kingship of David has been idealized in Jewish tradition. David himself was undoubtedly a charismatic figure; through his anointing, it was said that the spirit of the Lord came mightily upon him (I Samuel

16:13) and the biblical records chronicle his extraordinary triumphs. It was he who captured the city of Jerusalem from the Canaanites and established it as the capital of the united kingdom. He made it his administrative centre and built new fortifications and a palace – the Ark of the Covenant was brought there in state. Jerusalem had never been a tribal city, but it was David's city and it became not only the seat of government, but also the headquarters of the cult of the Israelite God. David also extended his territory by inflicting defeats on the Moabites, the Edomites, the Ammonites, the Syrians and the Phoenicians.

Yet he himself was far from perfect. For stealing Bathsheba, the wife of one of his soldiers, he was severely reproved by Nathan, one of the court prophets. According to II Samuel 7, God, speaking through Nathan, had already established a covenant with David: 'Your house and your kingdom shall be made sure for ever before me; your throne shall be established forever.' Although many kings of the ancient world saw themselves as the incarnation of their country's god, the covenant with David made it clear that the Israelite king ruled under God, and he too must keep God's laws. In punishment, the first son born to David and Bathsheba died. Their next child, Solomon, succeeded David as king.

King Solomon is primarily remembered for his wisdom and for building the Temple in Jerusalem. The Temple may have been designed to house the Ark of the Covenant, but its plan was very similar to that of other Canaanite temples that have been excavated in Israel. It was built of the most beautiful and costly materials, and its presence re-inforced Jerusalem's status as the cultic centre of the land.

But despite the king's reputed wisdom, there is no doubt that he alienated his people. He consolidated his extensive diplomacy by marrying foreign princesses, who brought their idolatrous religious practices with them to Jerusalem. He exacted taxes from his subjects to pay for his administration, his standing army and his court and, ultimately, he also demanded forced labour from the tribes. There is an ambiguity about the figure of Solomon; by worldly standards he was outstandingly successful – he made his realm a significant power in the ancient Middle East, extended his kingdom and provided splendid cultural and artistic opportunities – yet the seeds for the subsequent dissolution of the union were sown in his reign. The northern tribes in particular were restive. Despite the covenant with his father David, Solomon had failed to respond fully to the ethical demands of the God of Moses and the Patriarchs, and the consequences would be disastrous.

3. THE DIVIDED MONARCHY

After the death of Solomon in 928 BCE, his son Rehoboam was acclaimed as king by the two southern tribes, Judah and Benjamin, but the northern tribes would only acknowledge his kingship under certain conditions that Rehoboam was not prepared to meet. In consequence the northern tribes rebelled against the house of David and chose a military leader, Jeroboam, to be their king.

Initially Jeroboam made his capital at Shechem, but subsequently he removed it to Tirzah. The northern tribes did feel the loss of the Temple, but to discourage pilgrimage to the south, Jeroboam reactivated the old Canaanite shrines of Bethel and Dan and he seems to have set up altars with statues of golden bulls. The statues could have been interpreted as thrones for the Israelite God, but a bull was also the symbol for Baal, and the king's choice indicates a serious concession to the religion of the Canaanites. The second book of Kings describes the religious activities of the Northern Kingdom. The writer was much influenced by the laws of Deuteronomy (he is often called the Deuteronomic historian) and he condemns Jeroboam and his successors unequivocally for turning the people away from the Temple in Jerusalem and for worshipping at an idolatrous shrine.

Jeroboam's throne was unstable. His son succeeded him for a few months, but was toppled by Baasha, who ruled from 906 to 883. Again Baasha's son succeeded him, but he was assassinated by Zimri, who reigned only for seven days – in his turn he was replaced by Omri (882–871 BCE). The book of Kings tells us very little about King Omri, although we know from archaeological evidence that he forged successful foreign alliances, made peace with the southern tribes and married his son Ahab to the daughter of the powerful King of Phoenicia. He also built his own capital, the new city of Samaria. He was succeeded peacefully by his son Ahab, and here the biblical record becomes far more detailed. Ahab's Phoenician wife, Jezebel, seems to have been a devoted follower of Baal and encouraged the king to emulate her. At this point the mighty figure of Elijah enters the story. According to II Kings 17–19 and 21, he stood up to the king, condemned the Northern Kingdom to three years of drought, challenged the prophets of Baal to a trial of God's strength and, like the prophet Nathan before him, condemned the king for putting himself above the law in the matter of Naboth's vineyard. Elijah never died. Ultimately he was taken up to

Heaven in a fiery chariot (II Kings 1) and one day, the Jews believe, he will return to the earth to herald the messianic age.

Ahab survived, but the army general Jehu rebelled against Ahab's son, Joram. Jehu was anointed king by one of the prophetic followers of Elisha, the successor of Elijah, and he seems to have made some attempt to purge the Northern Kingdom of Baal worship. At this time the Assyrian empire in the east was expanding, and on the famous Black Obelisk of the Assyrian king, Shalmanezer (c. 840 BCE), Jehu is portrayed as bowing down before the Assyrian king, offering him gifts. Subsequently, under Jehu's son Jehoahaz (815–801), the Northern Kingdom came under the domination of Syria, but when Syria was conquered by Assyria the Northern Kingdom regained a measure of independence.

Under Jeroboam II (786–746) splendid buildings were constructed in Samaria and there is evidence of real prosperity. It was during this period that the first writing prophet, Amos, condemned the selfishness and self-indulgence of the rich. The people were religious – they worshipped God at the altars of Bethel and Gilgal – but the prophet maintained that ritual was meaningless without justice and righteous conduct: 'I hate, I despise your feasts, and I take no delight in your solemn assemblies . . . But let justice roll down like waters, and righteousness like an everflowing stream' (Amos 5:21–24).

Meanwhile the tribes of Judah and Benjamin in the Southern Kingdom remained loyal to the house of David, and Jerusalem remained within its territory. The second book of Kings gives the impression that Judah was by far the more important of the two kingdoms, but in fact it was smaller, poorer and probably less civilized. King Rehoboam was forced to pay tribute to the King of Egypt and, until the time of Omri, there were constant petty conflicts with the northern tribes. During the reign of King Uzziah (783–742), Judah's territory was extended and, as in the Northern Kingdom, there was a time of prosperity and peace. But the storm clouds were gathering. Under Tiglath Pilesar III (744–724) the Assyrians were pursuing a policy of expansion and imperialism.

4. THE END OF THE NORTHERN KINGDOM

In order to expand the Assyrian empire, Tiglath Pilesar III pursued a policy not merely of extracting tribute from conquered kings, but of relocating segments of the population to other areas of his empire. From c. 740 BCE, King Menahem of the Northern Kingdom was paying regular tribute to the Assyrians. Subsequently, after a palace revolution put King Pekah on the throne, anti-Assyrian alliances were formed with the Syrians. In 732 Pekah was assassinated by Hoshea who surrendered to the Syrians, but was soon plotting with the Egyptians. The political turmoil of the time is reflected in the words of the Israelite prophet Hosea when he declares, 'The corruption of Ephraim is revealed and the wicked deeds of Samaria . . . they devour their rulers. All their kings have fallen; and none of them calls upon me' (Hosea 7:7).

In 724 BCE, in retaliation for the Egyptian alliance, the Assyrian king attacked the Northern Kingdom, and the city of Samaria fell after a two-year siege. In the Assyrian Chronicles, King Sargon II described how more than 27,000 people were deported from the land of Israel and were replaced by foreigners. The ten northern tribes were decimated and the country was put under the care of an Assyrian governor.

The unknown fate of the ten northern tribes has been a subject of much conjecture over the centuries. The obvious explanation for their disappearance from history is that they intermarried with their new host population and lost their separate identity. This theory is not satisfactory, however, for many Christians and Jews. The ten tribes were a major segment of the people through whom God's promises to the Patriarch Abraham were to be fulfilled, and it is unthinkable that they no longer exist. Some time in the glorious future, in the days of the Messiah, many believe all twelve tribes will be restored once more to the Promised Land.

The rabbis of the talmudic period taught that the lost tribes lived beyond the river of Sambatyon somewhere in Arabia – a river with such a swift current that it could never be crossed. On the Sabbath it was still, but of course in obedience to Sabbath law, the ten tribes could not travel on the seventh day! In the Middle Ages, travellers told tales of having heard news of the tribes and certain groups have at different times been identified as their descendants. The Bene Israel of Bombay claim that their ancestors were shipwrecked when fleeing from the Assyrians; certain American Indian groups were thought to speak Hebrew and it was rumoured that they were descendants from the tribe of Reuben; the Falashas of Ethiopia claim to be members of the tribe of Dan and there have even been attempts to prove that the English-speaking peoples are really of Israelite descent. In any event, the loss of the ten northern tribes was a serious blow and for many generations the hope expressed by the sixth-century prophet Ezekiel was kept alive: 'Thus says the Lord God: "Behold I will take the people of Israel from the nations among which they have gone, and will gather them from all sides and bring them to their own land; and I will make them one nation in the Land . . . and they shall be my people and I will be their God"' (Ezekiel 37:21–23).

Meanwhile, against the advice of the prophet Isaiah, King Ahaz of the Southern Kingdom paid homage to the Assyrian king. He even went so far as to set up an Assyrian altar in the Temple in Jerusalem and offer sacrifices there as a sign of his submission. Much of the territory of Judah was lost at this time; there was economic recession and a flood of refugees arrived from the Northern Kingdom in need of housing and support. The prophets of the late eighth century, Hosea, Isaiah and Micah, all pronounced the same message: the people were sharply condemned for their selfishness and injustice. In those troubled times they were lulled into a false sense of security by their many sacrifices and their attention to religious observance, and Micah's condemnation resounds down the ages: 'Will the Lord be pleased with thousands of rams, with ten thousand rivers of oil? Shall I give my first-born for my transgression, the fruit of my body for the sins of my soul? He has shown you, O man, what is good and what does the Lord require of you but to do justice and to love kindness and to walk humbly with your God?' (Micah 6:7–8).

5. THE BABYLONIAN CONQUEST

The Assyrians remained the dominant power in the ancient Middle East until the late seventh century BCE. King Hezekiah of the Southern Kingdom, who succeeded his father Ahaz, initially resisted the temptation to plot with the Egyptians against Assyria, but he did remove the paraphernalia of Assyrian and Canaanite worship from the Temple. After the death of King Sargon of Assyria, he rebelled, but Sargon's successor Sennacharib marched into Judah and compelled Hezekiah to pay substantial tribute. In the words of the Assyrian Annals, he shut Hezekiah within the walls of his capital city 'like a bird in a cage'.

Hezekiah's successors submitted to the power of Assyria. Only when other parts of the empire began to break away in the late seventh century did Hezekiah's great-grandson Josiah begin to assert his independence.

Like Hezekiah, he reformed the worship of the Temple and asserted the centrality of the Jerusalem shrine. During his reign, a version of the book of Deuteronomy (see Chapter 2, Part 4) was discovered and provided the impetus for a thorough cleansing of the cult. At the same time Josiah succeeded in expanding the boundaries of the Southern Kingdom, and he seems to have controlled territory as far north as Galilee and land east of the River Jordan.

Meanwhile the King of Babylon was stirring. By 609 BCE, the Babylonians had defeated the Assyrians and in 605 they also defeated the Egyptians at the Battle of Carchemish. Inevitably the new king of Judah, Jehoiakim, tried to reassert the independence of the Southern Kingdom, but King Nebuchadnezzar of Babylon invaded Judah. He laid siege to Jerusalem and captured it in 597 BCE. Jehoiakim died during the course of the siege, but his son Jehoiachin was taken captive to Babylon and a new king, Zedekiah, was nominated by Nebuchadnezzar. These events are chronicled at the end of the second book of Kings and in the writings of the prophet Jeremiah.

Jeremiah's prophecy covers the years from c. 622 BCE until after the Babylonian invasion. Like the earlier prophets, he condemned the people's reliance on formal religious ritual. He was brought to trial, beaten, put in the stocks and forbidden to prophesy in public, but he continued to speak out. He was convinced that the Temple would be destroyed and Jerusalem would be reduced to a ruin: 'Thus says the Lord of Hosts: so will I break this people and this city as one breaks a potter's vessel, so that it can never be mended' (Jeremiah 19:11). Later, when King Jehoiachin and the leading citizens of Jerusalem had been taken into exile in Babylon, he compared them to good figs. The people who were left behind were the bad figs who would suffer the same fate as rotten fruit (Jeremiah 24).

The new king, Zedekiah, did not learn from his predecessor's mistakes. Aided by the Egyptians he rebelled against the Babylonians, and in retaliation King Nebuchadnezzar again laid siege to Jerusalem and, when the walls were breached, systematically destroyed all the major buildings of the city including the Temple. Zedekiah himself was blinded and taken in chains to Babylon.

The situation is poignantly conjured up in the Lachish letters. Lachish was a city to the south-west of Jerusalem, and here archaeologists have discovered scraps of broken pottery with messages written on them, seemingly to be addressed to a certain Yaush, who was probably the military commander of the city. They reflect a desperate state of affairs. According to Jeremiah 34:7, the Babylonian army was attacking not only Jerusalem, but also Lachish and Azekah, 'for these were the only fortified cities of Judah that were left'. The Lachish letters indicate that Azekah had already fallen. The writer reports, 'We are watching for the signals of Lachish . . . for we cannot see Azekah'.

There was a further deportation of the inhabitants of Judah in 582 BCE – Jeremiah himself had earlier been forced by his friends to flee to Egypt. For the next forty years the land lay desolate. As the book of Lamentations described it, 'How lonely sits the city that was full of people. . . . Judah has gone into exile because of affliction . . . she dwells now among the nations, but finds no resting place' (Lamentations 1:1–3). Although Jeremiah's worst predictions had come true, he never lost his faith in God but looked beyond the disaster and promised that God would give His people a 'new covenant'. He insisted that the day would come when God would not only demand obedience, but would give the Jews the power to be obedient. 'I will put my law within them and I will write it upon their hearts; and I will be their God and they will be my people' (Jeremiah 31:33).

SUGGESTED FURTHER READING

J. Gray, *The Biblical Doctrine of the Reign of God*, T. and T. Clark, 1979.
E.H. Heaton, *A Short Introduction to the Old Testament Prophets*, Oneworld Publications, 1996.
A.D.H. Mayes, *Israel in the Period of the Judges*, SCM, 1974.
H. Mouvley, *Guide to Old Testament Prophecy*, Lutterworth, 1979.

4 FROM RESTORATION TO DESTRUCTION

1. EXILE

Exile (in Hebrew 'galut') is a fundamental concept for the Jews. Throughout their long history, from the destruction of Solomon's Temple in 586 BCE, probably the majority of the community has lived in exile. The Babylonian exile itself officially ended when Babylonia was conquered by Persia; the Persians had a different attitude towards conquered people and allowed the Jews to return to Canaan in 538 BCE. Nonetheless, many Jews chose to stay and within 500 years Jewish colonies were to be found in all the major urban centres around the Mediterranean Sea and throughout Babylonia and Persia. These small communities were nurtured by institutions that had first been created in response to the Babylonian captivity.

The loss of the Temple in Jerusalem was devastating; the inhabitants of Judah had believed that God would protect the house of David for ever. The sense of loss is reflected in the poetry of the book of Lamentations and in some of the Psalms: 'By the waters of Babylon there we sat down and wept when we remembered Zion . . . How shall we sing the Lord's song in a foreign land? If I forget you O Jerusalem, let my right hand wither . . . ' (Psalm 137). Probably the books of Joshua, Judges, Samuel and Kings were composed during this period. Not only are they a record of Jewish history, but they also provide an explanation for the calamity. Israel was not faithful to her covenant relationship with God as spelled out in the book of Deuteronomy and therefore disaster was inevitable. Nonetheless the history ends on a note of hope – the last King of Judah, Jehoiachin, is released from prison. The Deuteronomic promise is preserved, despite the people's disobedience; in tribulation they would return to God, and God is merciful, 'He will not fail you or destroy you or forget the covenant with your fathers' (Deuteronomy 4:25–31).

It is probable that life for the exiles in Babylon was quite prosperous. According to the book of Ezra, when the exiles returned to Judah they were able to make substantial financial gifts towards the rebuilding of the Temple. The religious life of the people was sustained by such prophets as Ezekiel and Isaiah of Babylon. Ezekiel, in particular, stressed the need for personal righteousness and encouraged his listeners to look for the restoration of Zion, the reassembling of the tribes and the rebuilding of the Temple in Jerusalem. At the same time there is an acknowledgement that God has provided another sanctuary for the people in their dispersion (see Ezekiel 11:16) and this was widely understood by the later rabbis to be a reference to the synagogue.

The Babylonian exiles seem to have met together on a regular basis for prayer and the exposition of scripture. No sacrifices could be offered, because Jerusalem was the only proper place for sacrifice, and there was no need therefore for priests or Levites in the service; learned laymen could read from the holy books and lead the prayers. The synagogue became a house of study, a place for discussion, a community centre and a religious resource. We have little firm evidence about its development as an institution, but by the end of the Second Temple period, the synagogue was well established both in Israel and in the Dispersion. Most scholars believe it had its origin during the time of the Babylonian captivity. What is undisputed is that it was the synagogue that enabled the Jewish religion to survive the tragedies and vicissitudes that have befallen the Hebrew people.

After the death of the Babylonian King Nebuchadnezzar in 562 BCE, the Babylonian empire was ruled by a series of weak kings. By 539 BCE, Cyrus, King of Persia, emerged as the most powerful leader of the ancient Middle East. The old policies were reversed and the Jews were allowed to return to their own land. These momentous events are reflected in the prophecies that appear in the latter part of the book of Isaiah (Chapters 40–55). The fall of Jerusalem is described as occurring in the past and the prophet looks forward to the imminent fall of Babylon. Cyrus is mentioned by name as the instrument through whom God would restore His people to Jerusalem, when the Jews would become the light to all the nations so that God's salvation would eventually reach to the ends of the earth (Isaiah 44:28 and 49:6).

2. RETURN AND RENEWAL

The history of the return from Babylon is not entirely clear. In c. 538 BCE, the Persians appointed a governor for Judah named Sheshbazzar who started rebuilding the foundations of the Temple. Subsequently the work was continued by Joshua, a priest, and Zerubbabel, the grandson of the last king of Judah, Jehoiachin. They were encouraged in their activities by the prophets Haggai and Zechariah. Both prophets saw a special place for Zerubbabel in God's scheme of things and there are hints that Joshua, as High Priest of the people, also had an exalted role. The exact meaning of the prophecies is obscure, but from this period we can see the beginnings of a messianic hope – the belief that another Davidic king would emerge who would right all wrongs and establish God's kingdom on earth.

Even after the Temple had been destroyed, pilgrimages had been made to the site – not all the people of Judah had been taken into exile, and there were also some surviving descendants of the citizens of the Northern Kingdom. These offered to help Zerubbabel in the rebuilding, but their assistance was refused, because their Jewish origin was felt to be uncertain. The problem of the relationship between the returning exiles and the so-called 'people of the land' continued to haunt the Jewish leaders. Even after the Temple was rebuilt, the prophet Malachi, writing approximately sixty years after the return from Babylon, condemned the people for neglecting their religious duties and for 'marrying the daughter of a foreign god' (Malachi 2:11).

Nehemiah was appointed governor of Judah in 445 BCE, and he strongly condemned the links the Jewish people had formed with the inhabitants of Samaria (the old Northern Kingdom). The exact relationship between Nehemiah and the scribe Ezra is not clear. According to the book of Ezra, Ezra arrived in Jerusalem thirteen years before Nehemiah, but various factors make that unlikely. In any event, the two shared the same objectives. Ezra is described as the 'priest, the scribe, learned in matters of the commandments of the Lord and His statutes for Israel' (Ezra 7:11). He gathered the people together and read the law (probably the Pentateuch) to them. By this stage most of them could no longer understand Hebrew so, as it was read, it had to be translated into Aramaic, the official language of the Persian empire.

The people of Jerusalem were transfixed by the reading. They were determined to celebrate the festivals of Pesah (Passover), Shavuot

(Weeks) and Sukkot (Tabernacles) as prescribed in the law. These were agricultural festivals as well as commemorations of God's graciousness to the Jews in liberating them from slavery, giving them the Torah and preserving them in the wilderness. In addition, Ezra insisted that the people divorce their foreign wives and only marry within their own group; the people of Samaria were not to be allowed to worship in Jerusalem and the Jews were to remain a separate nation. It is possible that not everyone accepted this ethnic exclusivism, and some scholars believe that both the book of Ruth (in which a Moabite woman becomes the great-grandmother of King David) and the book of Jonah (in which God takes pity on the Assyrian capital Nineveh) were written in protest against Ezra's policy. Nonetheless the Jewish people owe their survival to their aversion to intermarriage and their refusal to be dissolved into other racial groups.

The people of Samaria saw that they were not to be accepted as true Israelites despite their opinion that they too were the legitimate heirs of the Patriarchs and Moses. Over the centuries they developed their own traditions, and they maintain to this day that their version of the Torah is the true one and that their High Priest is descended from the family of Aaron. In 333 BCE they were given permission to build their own Temple on Mount Gerizim and, though the building has long since been destroyed, the small surviving Samaritan community still offers a Passover sacrifice every year on that mountain.

Also in 333 BCE, King Darius of Persia was defeated by the young King Alexander of Macedon. Alexander conquered a vast empire including Egypt, Greece, Asia Minor, Persia, Babylon and land as far east as the borders of India. Everywhere he was determined to establish cities and spread Greek culture. When Alexander died in 323 BCE, Judah was at first placed under the control of the Egyptian leader Ptolemy, who was tolerant of Jewish religious practice, although he did encourage many Jews to emigrate to the new city of Alexandria on the Nile delta. There grew up a highly successful Greek-speaking Jewish community in that city, and it was there that the Bible was first translated into Greek, in the translation known as the Septuagint.

3. THE MACCABEAN REVOLT AND ITS AFTERMATH

By 198 BCE, the King of Asia Minor, Aristobulus III, had taken over the territory of Judah (or Judea as it came to be called in Greek). He was descended from one of Alexander's generals Seleucus, hence his line was known as 'Seleucid'. While Judea was dominated by the Seleucid kings in the second century, an attempt was made to Hellenize Jerusalem, with such innovations as Greek games being introduced. These involved athletes competing naked, and were abhorrent to pious Jews. Antiochus IV, known as Antiochus Epiphanes (175–163 BCE) not only robbed the Jerusalem Temple; he banned circumcision, the observance of the Sabbath and the reading of the Torah. In addition he announced that the Temple was to be rededicated to the Greek god Zeus, that sacrifice should include the offering of pigs and that gentiles (non-Jews) should also use the Temple for worship.

The Jews were outraged, and led by the priest Mattathias, they rose in open revolt. After Mattathias' death, his sons, particularly Judas (known as Maccabee, the hammer) took over the leadership of the rebellion, which is described in the books of Maccabees in the Apocrypha. After the Seleucids had slaughtered a group of Jews who refused to fight on the Sabbath, the whole country was in uproar. In 164 BCE, Judas' family, the Hasmoneans, succeeded in recapturing Jerusalem, cleansed the Temple, and dedicated it to God. The winter festival of Hanukkah (Lights) commemorates these events; supposedly there was only enough sacred oil for one night, but miraculously it lasted for eight, and still today members of the Jewish community light candles for eight days to celebrate the survival of their faith against the forces of Hellenism.

The Hasmonean family succeeded in founding a dynasty of both rulers and priests. When Judas was killed in 160 BCE, his brother Jonathan became High Priest, even though he was not of the priestly dynasty, and he was later recognized as governor of Judea. He was in turn succeeded by his brother Simon, who compelled the Seleucids to acknowledge Judea's independence and who took on the hereditary title of Ethnarch. When Simon was assassinated in 135 BCE, his son John Hyrcanus I became both Ethnarch and High Priest. He extended the kingdom to include Idumea, where he forced the inhabitants to convert to Judaism and also destroyed the Samaritans' Temple on Mount Gerizim. One of his sons, Aristobulus I (who ruled 104–103 BCE) conquered the region of Galilee and another, Alexander Jannaeus (102–76 BCE) occupied northern Trans-Jordan and the coastal cities of the Mediterranean.

However, by the middle of the first century BCE, the Roman general Pompey had annexed Syria and turned Judea into a client-state of the

Roman empire. John Hyrcanus II, the son of Alexander Jannaeus, took over as Ethnarch, and an Idumean leader, Antipater, was given special powers in Jerusalem. Subsequently, after a period of turmoil following the death of Julius Caesar, Antipater's son Herod laid siege with a Roman army to Jerusalem and conquered Judea in 37 BCE.

Herod was extremely unpopular. As an Idumean and thus the descendant of a convert to Judaism, he was not eligible for the High Priesthood. Instead he nominated a Babylonian Jew who was said to be descended from David's High Priest, Zadok, in preference to another Hasmonean. He executed many of the Jewish leaders who had been loyal to the Hasmonean family and, although he married Mariamne, a Hasmonean princess, he later put her to death for plotting against him.

Throughout his long reign, Herod supported the Roman Emperor. He built the port of Caesarea in honour of his master; he established a Greek amphitheatre in Jerusalem and built new fortifications in Jericho, in Herodium near Jerusalem, and at Masada overlooking the Dead Sea. He also worked for the betterment of his countrymen, negotiated with the Romans to preserve Jewish privileges in the Greek cities of the Dispersion, and rebuilt the Temple in Jerusalem on a sumptuous scale. It included a large court for the gentiles, an inner court for Jewish women and a court of priests where the daily sacrifices were offered. The inmost sanctum was the Holy of Holies, veiled by a curtain, which was only entered once a year when the High Priest prayed for the forgiveness of the people on Yom Kippur (the Day of Atonement). Despite all these efforts, Herod was hated as a tyrant and a traitor, and died unlamented in 4 BCE.

4. PHARISEES, SADDUCEES AND ESSENES

During the Hasmonean period various sects appeared among the Jews of Judea, which we know about from the writings of Josephus, a Jewish historian of the first century CE. The discovery of the Dead Sea Scrolls has also given us further knowledge of one particular Essene-like sect, and the Pharisees and Sadducees are mentioned in the Christian New Testament. It must be remembered however that the New Testament gives a very negative picture of Jews and Judaism; it does not explain what, if any, ideological differences existed between the two groups and the whole Jewish establishment is portrayed as the unenlightened background against which the person of Jesus emerges as saviour of humanity. Against this account should be placed the mass of rabbinic literature in which the discussions of the Pharisees are recorded and preserved.

The Sadducees have left no records of their own, so we only see them through the eyes of their opponents. They were a small group that included the hereditary priests who controlled the worship in the Temple. Their leader was the High Priest. The name 'Sadducee' may well derive from Zadok, King David's High Priest. They had a distinctive religious position; although they upheld the complete authority of the written law (the five books of Moses), they did not accept the validity of the oral interpretation of the law. Consequently they rejected such doctrines as the resurrection of the dead, which had developed as a result of discussing the implications of the scriptural text. The Sadducees' religion centred on the cycle of Temple worship, with its daily sacrifices and annual festivals. As the hereditary aristocrats of the Jewish people, they collaborated with the government in order to preserve their religious institutions and their influence was out of all proportion to their numbers.

Josephus indicates that the Pharisees enjoyed the support of the multitude of the Jews. Their leaders are described as sages and scribes and they were essentially laymen. They were deeply involved in the interpretation of Scripture and their prestige lay in their dedication to the study of the complexity of the fast-developing oral law. They had no desire to destroy the Temple and the Priesthood – both were believed to have been given by God – but they saw themselves as the successors of Moses, as the moral leaders of the people. They regarded the High Priest and his deputies as having primarily ceremonial duties; they were not the source of wisdom or ethical teaching.

The platform of the Pharisees was the synagogue. By the first century BCE, every village in Judea had a synagogue where the community would gather to hear the reading of the law and listen to the Pharisaic expositions. The Pharisees did not object to the monarchy; only when the Roman governors and Jewish puppet-kings outraged Jewish sensibilities did they adopt a policy of resistance. Nevertheless, as the Romans tightened their grip on the province of Judea, the Pharisees came increasingly to hope for the restoration of an independent Jewish state under God's anointed king, the Messiah.

Josephus also describes a monastic group known as the Essenes, who are also mentioned by Philo of Alexandria and the Roman writer Pliny. They seem to have withdrawn themselves from society, lived in separate groups and held all goods in common. The sect of Qumran, which produced the Dead Sea Scrolls, shared many of the characteristics described by Josephus. They seem to have been inspired by a vision of the Last Days, which they believed were soon to dawn. They regarded themselves as the faithful remnant, the last righteous ones of Israel, and they disapproved of both the Pharisees and the Sadducees as corrupt compromisers.

The Sanhedrin was the supreme religious body of the Jews of this period and it was composed of both Pharisees and Sadducees. Mentioned in the New Testament, its exact nature and function are unclear. The Great Sanhedrin of Jerusalem apparently consisted of seventy-one members and met in the Hall of Hewn Stones in the Temple. Under the Hasmoneans the Sanhedrin had considerable political influence, but from the reign of King Herod onwards its discussions were confined to religious matters. Its two senior officials were known as the Nasi ('Prince') and the Av Bet Din ('Father of the Court').

5. THE JEWISH WAR

After the death of Herod in 4 BCE, his kingdom was divided between his three sons. Ten years later, however, one of the sons, Archelaus, was exiled by the Romans and Judea became a Roman province ruled by a procurator. There was continual discontent among the Jews. When the Romans took a census of the population, which was contrary to Jewish law, resistance became active and there are records of several small-scale messianic movements. Jesus of Nazareth was one who spread his message during this period. Of all the procurators, Pontius Pilate, who plays an important part in the New Testament, was particularly insensitive to the Jews. He brought Roman standards with the Emperor's insignia into the Holy City and used Jewish religious funds to pay for a new aqueduct.

There was a short respite during the reign of the Emperor Claudius (CE 41–54). He gave Judea the status of a self-governing kingdom under King Agrippa I, but at Agrippa's death in CE 44, the country returned to the status of a province. There was considerable hostility between the rich and the poor; prophets and holy men roamed the countryside; there was a terrible famine between CE 46 and 48, and an increased atmosphere of messianic excitement. This was the era of the rise of the Zealots. According to Josephus, the Zealots had been organized by one Judas of Galilee during the reign of Herod, and were not only fanatical nationalists, they were also dedicated to God and His Torah. They believed that God had given the land of Canaan to His chosen people, and the presence of the heathen Romans in the Promised Land was a defilement and a sacrilege. A Zealot is numbered among Jesus' disciples, and the influence of the Zealot party increased after CE 44. The later procurators were men of little sympathy and they continually outraged Jewish religious sensibilities. The Sadducees continued to try to co-operate with the occupying power, and many of the Pharisees were men of peace, but the people could not be held back for ever.

Matters came to a head in CE 66. A small Roman legion and a group of pro-Roman Jews were killed in a popular uprising led by the Zealots. The Roman governor marched on Jerusalem, but was driven back to the coast; then a superior Roman army was assembled in the north and laid siege to the fortress of Jotapata. Meanwhile the Zealots had overthrown the moderate government in Jerusalem and the Roman general Vespasian marched south, subjugating Idumea, Western Judea, Samaria and Jericho. In CE 70, Vespasian's son, Titus, was put in charge of the campaign, and he laid siege to the city of Jerusalem. By late May, the newer part of Jerusalem was in Roman hands, and at the end of July the Romans captured the citadel next to the Temple. On 6 August the daily sacrifices were suspended and on 28 August the entire Temple went up in flames.

By the end of September, Jerusalem was completely under Roman control and Titus ordered that the city should be devastated. All that remained standing of Herod's great Temple was the extreme western wall (the Wailing Wall). In accordance with their customs, Vespasian and Titus led a triumphal procession through Rome displaying Jewish captives taken in the siege, and ceremonial objects looted from the Temple. The Arch of Titus was built in Rome to commemorate the occasion; the arch's frieze portrays Roman soldiers pillaging the Temple and taking away the great golden seven-branched candlesticks.

The Roman task was not yet complete. The rebels had fled south and had taken possession of Herod's fortress of Masada, overlooking the Dead Sea. Despite the small numbers involved, the Romans put enormous resources into laying a siege and the fortress eventually fell in

CE 74. Josephus vividly describes the end of the Zealots who, on the eve of the final battle, chose to commit suicide rather than fall into the hands of the enemy. The speech of the rebel leader has proved an inspiration for generations of Jewish freedom fighters, and since the founding of the state of Israel in 1948, the Israeli government has been determined that Masada must not fall again.

SUGGESTED FURTHER READING

R.J. Coggins, *Samaritans and Jews*, Blackwell, 1975.
Josephus, *The Jewish War*, Penguin, 1959.
H. Maccoby, *Judaism in the First Century*, Sheldon Press, 1989.
D.S. Russell, *The Jews from Alexander to Herod*, Oxford, 1967.

5 RABBINIC JUDAISM

1. THE ACADEMY AT JAVNEH

The destruction of the Temple was an unimaginable catastrophe. There could be no more daily sacrifices, since the Temple was the only legitimate location for sacrifice; thus there was no central focus for the Jewish people. The hereditary priests, the Sadducees, had lost their role in the community. Over the centuries many of their descendants retained the memory of their ancient glory and to this day some Jews are labelled 'kohenim' (priests) and are subject to certain ritual restrictions. With the Temple a charred ruin, Judaism could have disappeared like so many of the cults of the ancient world. The fact that it survived is due to the remarkable vision and persistence of the Pharisaic leaders of the time.

Rabban Johanan ben Zakkai (a pupil of Rabbi Hillel, the greatest of the sages of the Second Temple period) had managed to escape from Jerusalem during the siege. He settled in the town of Javneh near the coast and gathered around him a group of scholars known as the Tannaim. They occupied themselves with the development of the legal tradition. Under Johanan's successor, Rabban Gamaliel II, the Sanhedrin was re-established with Gamaliel himself as the Nasi and Rabbi Joshua as the Av Bet Din. This was recognized as the supreme Jewish representative body in both Judea and the Dispersion. Decisions were reached collectively after discussion, and scholars and students came from near and far to listen to and participate in the debate. It was during this period that the Canon of Scripture was determined, the regular daily prayers organized, a system of rabbinical ordination introduced and many of the old Temple rituals transferred to the synagogue. The past was not forgotten; the teachings of the early Pharisaic scholars from the late first century BCE and early first century CE, such as Hillel and his great contemporary Shammai, were summarized and the details of the Temple ritual were remembered and rehearsed so that all could one day be restored.

Among the distinguished sages of Javneh were Rabbis Eliezar ben Hyrcanus, Joshua ben Hanina, Tarphon and Ishmael ben Elisha. By the early second century CE, the most prominent scholar was Rabbi Akiva, who taught a particular method of scriptural exegesis (see Section 3) and who was also an eminent legal authority. Outside the land of Judea, Jewish uprisings continued to take place throughout the Roman Empire, particularly in Alexandria, Cyrene and Cyprus. In all the rebellions Jews were massacred. In CE 132 another messianic figure emerged in Israel. Simeon bar Kokhba (his name means 'son of a star' and was seen to fulfil Numbers 24:17, 'there shall step forth a star out of Jacob') seems to have been inspired by the belief that God would empower His people to regain their freedom and rebuild the Temple. The revolt lasted three years and was supported by Rabbi Akiva, who believed Simeon was the long-awaited Messiah. It was sparked off by the Emperor Hadrian's programme of Hellenization, and it was initially successful; Simeon's government minted coins and set up a system of country-wide deputies. But the might of Rome was too great. According to a later historian, hundreds and thousands of Jews were killed in the ensuing battles and the whole country was devastated. By CE 135, the final rebel stronghold, Bethar, to the south-west of Jerusalem, was captured. This was said to have occurred on the ninth day of the month of Av, the anniversary of the destruction of both Solomon's and Herod's Temples. It is still observed as a day of mourning in the Jewish community. Simeon himself was killed during the campaign and Rabbi Akiva was captured by the Romans and flayed alive. Jews were forbidden to live in the ruins of Jerusalem and a new Roman city was built on the site known as Aeolia Capitolina.

After the rebellion the practice of Judaism was outlawed in Judea, but this decree was rescinded in 138. There were no more attempts to rebel. The Jewish leaders now pursued a policy of conciliation towards their Roman overlords and the academy at Javneh was transferred to Galilee. Eminent scholars of the late second century include Rabbis Simeon ben Gamaliel II, Simeon bar Yohai and Meir. The Sanhedrin continued to flourish and succeeded in providing a focus for Jewish religious life.

2. THE MISHNAH

After peace was established with the Romans, the Nasi was entrusted with the collection of taxes, the appointment of judges for the Jewish community and the maintenance of contact with the communities outside Galilee. Judah Ha-Nasi, the son of Simeon ben Gamaliel II, not only performed these functions, but was also responsible for compiling the oral tradition into a book, the Mishnah. By the third century CE, oral interpretations of the law had become highly complex. There had been earlier attempts at codification, notably by Rabbi Akiva and Rabbi Meir, but the material had not been arranged according to its subject matter. What was needed was an authoritative record of the debates and decisions of the Tannaim on each particular topic.

Nearly 150 sages are mentioned by name in the text, dating from the time of Hillel and Shammai. The debates are recorded with the minority view expressed first and the final decision set down at the end. The usual formula is 'Rabbi Simeon says . . . but the sages declare . . . '. The text is divided into six orders. The first, Zeraim ('Seeds'), deals with benedictions and agricultural laws; the second, Mo'ed ('Fixed Seasons'), is concerned with the laws of the Sabbath, festival days and fast days; the third order, Nashim ('Women'), mainly covers the regulation of marriage and divorce; the fourth, Nezikin ('Damages'), is concerned with civil and criminal law including punishments and idolatry; the fifth, Kodashim ('Holy Matters'), discusses sacrifices and the ritual of the Temple; and the sixth, Tohorot ('Cleanliness'), deals with the laws of ritual purity.

The Mishnah is almost entirely halakhic (legal) in content. Each order contains a number of tractates and each tractate is divided into chapters. Altogether there are sixty-three tractates and 523 chapters.

The ninth tractate of the order of Nezikin is an exception. Known as the Pirke Avot ('Sayings of the Fathers'), it is printed in most editions of the Jewish Prayer Book, and unlike the rest of the Mishnah it does not deal with correct conduct in particular circumstances. Rather, it is a collection of rabbinic sayings and ethical advice. The text begins by establishing a chain of authority:

> Moses received the Torah ('Law') from Sinai and handed it down
> to Joshua, and Joshua to the elders, and the elders to the prophets
> and the prophets handed it down to the men of the Great

> Assembly . . . Simon the Just was one of the last survivors of the
> Great Assembly . . . Antigonos of Secho received the tradition
> from Simon the Just . . . Jose ben Joezar and Jose ben Jochanan
> received it from them . . . Joshua ben Perachiah and Nittai the
> Arbelite received it from them . . . Judah ben Tabbai and Simon
> ben Shetach received it from them . . . Shemaiah and Abtalion
> received it from them . . . Hillel and Shammai received it from
> them.

The chain continues through Rabban Gamaliel II, his son Simeon,
through Judah Ha-Nasi and finally through Judah's son Gamaliel.
Traditionally, Avot is read in the synagogue between the festivals of Pesah
and Shavuot, and it is undoubtedly the best known and best loved part of
the Mishnah. It is eminently quotable:

> Upon three things is the world based; upon Torah, upon service
> and upon the practice of charity . . .
> Be of the disciples of Aaron, loving peace and pursuing peace,
> loving your fellow-creatures and drawing them towards the
> Torah . . .
> If I am not for myself, who will be for me? And if I am for myself,
> who am I? And if not now, when? . . .
> The day is short and the task is great and the labourers are
> sluggish and the recompense is ample and the Master of the house
> is urgent.

The Mishnah does not include all the existing oral law. There is also a
parallel collection called the Tosefta ('Supplement') which again is
subdivided into six orders, with the same names as those of the
Mishnah. Different theories have been offered as to the exact relationship
between the two works, and it may be that the Tosefta is simply a more
extensive record of the sages' discussions. In addition, scattered through
the Palestinian and Babylonian Talmuds (see Part 5) are further sayings
of the Tannaim not included in the original Mishnah. Nonetheless,
the Mishnah is a remarkable piece of work. By codifying the morass of
oral law, Judah Ha-Nasi succeeded in providing a solid foundation
upon which further discussion and interpretation could be based.

3. RABBINIC INTERPRETATION OF SCRIPTURE

Besides the oral law, the Tannaim were also preoccupied with the
interpretation of the biblical text. Rabbinic interpretation of scripture is

known as 'midrash' and is of two main types. Direct exegesis involves comment on a particular passage of the Bible, while indirect exegesis uses a scriptural text to support a theological or halakhic concept. An example of direct exegesis might be a midrash on Deuteronomy 15:11, 'You shall open wide your hand to your brother'. This is explained as meaning that you should fulfil your brother's particular needs: 'To him for whom bread is suitable, give bread; to him who needs dough, give dough; to him for whom money is required, give money; to him for whom it is fitting to put food in his mouth, put it in.' Similarly the beginning of Psalm 50, 'The Mighty One, God, the Lord' is explained as 'only one name, even as one man can be called workman, builder, architect. The Psalmist mentions these three names to teach you that God created the world with three names, corresponding with three good attributes by which the world was created.' Here the rabbinic commentator is particularly anxious to disabuse the reader of the Christian idea that the three names might imply that God is a Trinity.

In rabbinical hermeneutics, it was a principle that words should always be understood in their most precise sense. So Rabbi Meir, in the second century CE, argued that because Exodus 15:1 is to be translated 'Then will Moses and then will the Children of Israel sing this song unto the Lord' (rather than 'Then did Moses and then did the Children of Israel sing this song') it must refer to some time in the future. Yet we know that Moses and the Israelites are long since dead, so clearly there must be a resurrection of the dead some time in the future if this passage is to be fulfilled. The same argument is applied by Rabbi Joshua to the text 'They will be praising thee' in Psalm 84.

Indirect exegesis begins from the ethical or theological injunction and works its way back to the original text. For example:

> When you are judging and there come before you two men, of
> whom one is rich and the other poor, do not say, 'The poor
> man's words are to be believed, but not the rich man's'. But just
> as you listen to the words of the poor man, so listen to the words
> of the rich man, for it is said, 'You shall not be partial in
> judgment'.
>
> (Deuteronomy 1:17)

Before the destruction of the Temple, Rabbi Hillel had laid down seven rules for biblical exegesis, which were expanded to thirteen by Rabbi Ishmael in the second century. These include the rule of the inference of the major from the minor. If a rule applies in a matter of minor importance, we must also suppose it is applicable in a case of major importance. So the Mishnah teaches that the Sabbath is more sacred than a common holiday; if an action should be avoided on an ordinary day, how much more important that it should be avoided on the Sabbath. Another rule is concerned with the reconciliation of contradictory passages in the text. If two passages say different things, if possible they should be reconciled by a third passage. So Exodus 13:6 declares that for the seven days of Passover you should eat unleavened bread, but Deuteronomy 16:8 demands only six days. This conflict can be resolved by referring to Leviticus 23:8, which maintains that the new corn may not be used until after the offering on the first day of Passover. Therefore the rabbis argue that the six days of Deuteronomy refer to the eating of unleavened bread made with the new corn, whereas the seven days of Exodus include one day of unleavened bread made with the old corn.

Rabbinic exegesis grew out of the conviction that the Bible is a sacred text and that it can provide a guide for daily living. Through following definite rules of interpretation and by careful, diligent study, God's will is revealed to His chosen people. The Tannaim and their successors the Amoraim produced extraordinary midrashic collections of stories, legends, parables, and ethical injunctions based on the biblical text. All reflect the fundamental belief that God's word as expressed in the Bible has a living message for each new generation.

4. THE ACADEMIES

After the Bar Kokhba revolt, under the leadership of the disciples of Rabbi Akiva, the Sanhedrin reassembled at Usha and later settled at the Roman city of Tiberias. Although the Nasi remained the leader of the Sanhedrin, other scholars founded their own academies elsewhere. They gathered students around them, taught, and applied the teachings of the Mishnah to their everyday lives. Other oral teachings, known as the Beraitot, were also preserved and expounded, and the success of each academy depended on the learning and fame of the central rabbi. Well-known academies in the land of Israel included those of Tiberias, Caesarea and Sepphoris.

Meanwhile Babylon had also become an important centre of Jewish life. There had been a community in Babylon since the time of the destruction of the First Temple in 586 BCE. By the second century CE, the ruler of Babylon, the King of Persia, had formally recognized a leader of the Jewish community, who was known as the Exilarch. This was an hereditary office and was traditionally thought to go back to the last king of Davidic descent, King Jehoiachin. The role of the Exilarch was not unlike that of the Nasi in Israel. He was responsible for the collection of taxes, the appointment of judges and for representing Jewry at the Persian court.

During and after the Bar Kokhba revolt in Israel, several scholars settled in Babylonia, bringing with them their habits of study and teaching. With their encouragement, a number of Babylonian Jews travelled to Israel to learn the oral law from the rabbis in the academies. Once the Mishnah had been codified, the scholars of Babylon and the scholars of Israel could be engaged in parallel studies. The Exilarch seems to have encouraged the emergence of an intelligentsia who could be entrusted with administrative and judicial duties. Thus, as the rabbis in Israel were discussing the application of the Mishnah to everyday life, so the scholars of Babylon were similarly engaged and there was constant communication between the two centres.

In about CE 219, the Babylonian scholar Rav (Abba bar Aviva), who had himself been a pupil of Judah Ha-Nasi in Israel, founded an academy at Sura in Central Mesopotamia, and this was to flourish for eight centuries. There was already an academy at Nehardia, presided over by Samuel, in the early third century. Many of Samuel and Rav's discussions are recorded in the Talmud (see Part 5). The Nehardia academy was destroyed in 259, but soon afterwards another academy was founded at Pumbedita in North Babylonia on the Euphrates river, and this was seen as the successor to Nehardia. Pumbedita was founded by Rabbi Judah, a student of Samuel, and it survived for seven hundred years. The two academies of Sura and Pumbedita were the leading places of Jewish learning in the Diaspora and were responsible for the training of many of the scholars mentioned in the Talmud.

Traditionally the scholars of Babylonia were not called 'Rabbi'. The title (meaning 'my master') had emerged as a mode of address for the sages of the Tannaitic period, after the time of Hillel and Shammai. It is mentioned ironically in the New Testament, when Jesus criticizes the Pharisees who love 'to be called by men, Rabbi' (Matthew 23:7). It was only granted to those who were properly ordained, and this was originally performed through the laying on of hands. Ordination was required for membership of the Sanhedrin and for those who acted as judges in criminal cases. It was, however, only granted to scholars who lived in Israel; so, for example, of the two sages Jonathan ben Akni and Simeon ben Zinid, only one was ordained, as the other had left Israel. In consequence the scholars of Babylonia were given the title 'Rav'. Among the famous Amoraim of Babylonia were Rav Ashi and Rav Avina of Sura (known as Ravina), and Rav Rabbah bar Nahmani, Joseph bar Hiyya, Abbaye and Rava of Pumbedita.

It should perhaps be pointed out that the modern title of Rabbi is used somewhat differently. The scholars of Israel and Babylonia were primarily interpreters and expounders of the Bible and the oral law; they were not full-time ministers with congregations. They almost invariably had other occupations from which they gained their livelihoods, and it was only in the Middle Ages that the title of Rabbi was revived to mean the spiritual leader of a particular Jewish community.

5. THE TALMUD

By the end of the fourth century, the Amoraim of Israel had gathered together the teachings of generations of rabbis in the academies. Four of the original six orders of Judah Ha-Nasi's Mishnah (Zeraim, Mo'ed, Nashim and Nezikin) provided the framework for further debate, explanation and interpretation. The additional material is known as 'Gemara', but we do not know how it was collated and put together. Most scholars believe that the Gemara on Nezikin was compiled earlier than that of the other three orders, but it may be that there was also Gemara on Kodashim and Tohorot, which is now lost. There are references to it in certain mediaeval texts, but no fragment has ever been found. The language of this work, known as the Palestinian Talmud, is Western Aramaic, and the book was compiled from the three major academies of Caesarea, Tiberias and Sepphoris. There was little attempt to smooth out the many contradictions and repetitions.

Similar activity took place in the academies of Babylonia. Rav Ashi of Sura began to compile the Gemara of Babylonia and the text of the Babylonian Talmud was completed in the sixth century. It is a massive work and, like the Palestinian Talmud, it records the discussions of the Amoraim on the Mishnah. It covers slightly fewer tractates than its Palestinian counterpart; very little of Zeraim and Tohorot is included, and several tractates from the other orders are missing. Nonetheless it is nearly four times as long, with approximately two-and-a-half million words. Its range is much broader and includes a great deal of aggadic (non-legal) material on such subjects as theology, folklore, legends, ethics and magic. It is written in Eastern Aramaic, and it is often compared with a great sea – there is no attempt at systematizing the discussion, extraneous matters are introduced and the debates often go off at a tangent. Material is not presented in a logical manner; the laws for writing a Torah scroll, for example, are recorded in the tractate on meal offerings in the Temple, and the regulations for the festival of Hanukkah are to be found in the tractate on the Sabbath.

The Babylonian Talmud reflects the daily life of the Jewish people of the fifth and sixth centuries CE. Not only does it provide laws for the guidance of the community, it gives us information about contemporary ideas on medicine, agriculture, botany, zoology, astronomy and history as well as on customs and superstitions. There are popular proverbs, fables, fairy-tales, moral maxims, prayers, rules of etiquette, spells and parables. The wisdom of the simple is recorded as well as the pronouncements of the sages, and there is a constant free association of ideas. Inevitably, when all manuscripts had to be copied by hand many errors crept in, and there are innumerable variant readings of the text. Nonetheless, as soon as it was compiled and written down, the Talmud became the authoritative text for teaching. It was the main study of the Babylonian academies and it spread throughout the Jewish world. To this day it remains the main text for study in the yeshivot (academies), the kollelim (higher academies) and in the batei ha-midrash (houses of study).

Although there were two Talmuds, the Babylonian version is accepted as the most authoritative. The Palestinian Talmud was compiled about 150 years before the Babylonian and there is a well-known halakhic (legal) principle that maintains the final decision should accord with the view of the later authority. So when the Palestinian and Babylonian

Talmuds contradict each other, the Babylonian version is to be followed. Also, the academies of Sura and Pumbedita in Babylonia became the most important centres for world Jewry. Baghdad was the capital of the Islamic world as the seat of the Caliph, and Jewish communities in the Diaspora turned to the Exilarch and the Gaonim (the heads of the academies) whose authority was accepted by the Muslim ruler. The importance of the Babylonian Talmud cannot be exaggerated in the history of the Jewish people. Even though many of the laws relating to the Temple and the sacrificial system were no longer applicable, they were studied with the same assiduity as the regulations concerning marriage and civil damages. The principle was one of 'Torah li-Shema' – studying the law for its own sake. All Jewish boys were expected to participate in this study, and the ideal was to be a scholar for whom it was a lifetime commitment.

SUGGESTED FURTHER READING

A. Cohen, *Everyman's Talmud*, Shocken, 1975.
C.H. Montefiore and H. Loewe, *A Rabbinic Anthology*, Shocken, 1974.
S. Schechter, *Aspects of Rabbinic Theology*, Shocken, 1961.
H. Strack, *Introduction to the Talmud and Midrash*, Jewish Publication Society, 1931.

6 THE DISPERSION

1. JEWS IN THE ROMAN EMPIRE

Jews had lived in Babylonia since the time of the Exile in the sixth century BCE. By the first century CE, there were also Jewish communities in the major cities of the Mediterranean. St Paul, in his Epistle to the Romans, speaks of visiting Spain (15:24) and since it was always his practice to preach Christianity first to the Jews, we must assume that there was a Jewish colony as far west as Spain. These communities did not always have an easy time. Because of their religious practices, the Jews lived apart from their pagan neighbours and were frequently regarded with hostility, although to some extent they were protected by their Roman overlords. They were not, for example, required to serve in the Roman army, because that would have meant violating the Sabbath.

At this time Judaism seems to have been a missionary religion. In the New Testament Jesus describes the Pharisees crossing 'sea and land to make a single proselyte' (Matthew 23:15). The rabbis taught that converts to Judaism must have exactly the same status as those born Jewish. In addition, the synagogues both in Israel and in the Dispersion seem to have attracted groups of gentiles who were unwilling to undergo the rite of circumcision, but who were sympathetic to Jewish religious practices. These were known as 'God-fearers' and they are mentioned in the Acts of the Apostles. In any event, the rabbis taught that any gentile who obeyed the fundamental laws of conduct given to Noah would have a place in the world to come.

In contrast, the emerging Christian Church was far less tolerant. Christianity had originally arisen as a sect within Judaism, and like such groups as the Essenes (see Chapter 4, Part 4), the early Christians believed themselves to have inherited the privileges of the true Israel. Mainstream Judaism was seen as corrupt, and the synagogue was thought to have abandoned its divinely inspired purpose. Jesus' teaching was contrasted with Jewish blindness and hard-heartedness, and the New Testament lays the blame for Jesus' death squarely on the Jewish community. Modern New Testament scholars have pointed out that the conflicts between Jesus and the Jewish leaders were almost certainly interpolated into the Gospel traditions for polemical reasons. In the early days, the Christian Church did contain a number of conservative Jews who wanted all new Christians to become fully observant Jewish proselytes, but increasingly the Christian Gospel spread beyond the Jewish community. Since the Jews remained faithful to the old covenant, God was considered to have rejected them and to have created a new Israel. By the time the Fourth Gospel was written, at the end of the first century CE, the split was complete. The Jews are portrayed as demonic – they sought to kill Jesus, who is the one true path to God. The seeds were sown for centuries of Christian anti-Semitism (see Part 5).

However, Christianity did not become the official religion of the Roman Empire until the fourth century CE. Meanwhile, the Jewish leaders tried to establish a harmonious relationship with the Romans, and there were some highly successful communities. For example, from the second century BCE until the middle of the first century CE, the Jews of Alexandria in North Africa were largely self-governing. Their central synagogue was famous for its splendour, the community was ruled over by an Ethnarch and had its own bet din (court). The Bible had been translated into Greek and there were Jewish poets, dramatists and historians. Most famous of all was the philosopher Philo (c. 25 BCE – 40 CE) who interpreted the Jewish Scriptures in the light of Hellenistic thought. Unfortunately, when the community tried to attain full civic rights, riots broke out and there were further disturbances in CE 66 in reaction to the Jewish war in Judea. These were suppressed by the Roman governor but the community never recovered its earlier prominence.

There was another large community in Rome. Jews were said to be conspicuous in mourning for Julius Caesar in 44 BCE. From the second half of the first century, the community seems to have been firmly established, and there is archaeological evidence of twelve synagogues, including one belonging to the Samaritans, and there are six Jewish catacombs yielding about five hundred inscriptions. With the Roman Emperor's adoption of Christianity in the fourth century, however, the position of Jews in the city changed dramatically for the worse.

2. JEWS UNDER EARLY ISLAMIC RULE

By the sixth century CE, Jews were largely a Diaspora people. Christianity had become the dominant religion of the Roman Empire and the Jews suffered various legal disadvantages. Imperial law forbade conversion to Judaism and intermarriage between Christians and Jews. From the beginning of the fifth century, Jews were officially barred from holding government positions. The land of Israel, as part of the Roman Empire, ceased to be a major centre of Jewish activity; Babylonia, on the other hand, was outside the influence of Rome and there the Jewish community prospered. The academies of Sura and Pumbedita in particular attained international prestige, attracted many students and, through special messengers, spread their decisions throughout the Jewish world.

At this time the Arab peoples of the Arabian peninsula were polytheists living either in urban centres or as nomadic tribes wandering from place to place. In the seventh century the Prophet Muhammad denounced the paganism of his countrymen, and claimed to have received a revelation from Allah, the One True God, which superseded the messages given to the biblical figures Abraham and Moses. The role of the ancient prophets had been to warn the people against idolatry, but Muhammad's revelation, the Qur'án, was received as the ultimate word of God. Initially Muhammad had hoped to convert the Jews to his vision, but the community refused to accept him, and he denounced the Jewish nation as infidels. He maintained that they had distorted Allah's message and that, although the Torah was divinely inspired, it was incomplete and needed to be read with the Qur'án in order to confirm, correct and fulfil it.

By CE 626, two Jewish tribes had been expelled from the city of Medina and a third had been exterminated. Muslim progress was astonishingly speedy, and by 644 Syria, Israel, Egypt, Iraq and Persia had become part of the new Islamic empire, ruled over by a Caliph. By the beginning of the eighth century, Muslim soldiers had crossed North Africa and the Straits of Gibraltar to conquer Spain.

The following century saw the flowering of Islamic learning: Muslim law, philosophy, theology, scriptural interpretation and science all flourished. It was also a period of toleration, in which both Jews and Christians were recognized as Peoples of the Book. Provided they accepted the supremacy of the Islamic state, they were guaranteed exemption from military service, and enjoyed judicial autonomy and religious toleration. This was officially codified in the Pact of Omar of c. 800. According to its provisions, however, Jews also suffered certain restrictions: they could not make converts, they had to pay an extra annual poll tax and they had to wear distinctive clothing. This of course had the effect of helping the community maintain its distinctive identity, and in general Jewish life prospered. Living in the urban centres of the empire, many became skilled craftsmen and, using their international contacts, they established extensive trading networks.

There was free movement of people throughout the empire, so Jews were able to establish new centres. They even carried their trading activities beyond the empire's boundaries. In the ninth century, Jewish merchants supposedly converted the king of the Khazar tribe (a Turkish people on the Volga river) to Judaism. The Muslim regime was welcomed by the Jews, because compared with the oppressive Christian legislation of Rome and the provinces of Byzantium, life in the Islamic empire was protected and relatively safe.

The Muslim leaders even confirmed the authority of the Babylonian institutions. When Babylonia was conquered, the Exilarch was again recognized as the leader of the Diaspora Jewish community and he was invited to represent his people at the court of the Caliph. He shared his power with the heads of the two talmudic academies who were known as the Gaonim (the Excellencies). These religious leaders were drawn from a small number of prominent Jewish families and, by the end of the eighth century, the Gaonim were claiming the right of appointing the Exilarch. Gradually the influence of the Exilarch declined, and the Gaonim established their power by delivering lectures on Jewish law and sending Responsa (answers) to halakhic enquiries throughout the Diaspora. By the beginning of the tenth century, the two academies had moved to Baghdad, the seat of the Caliphate, and the position of Exilarch had become largely honorific.

3. KARAISM

A threat to the unity of Diaspora Jewry was posed by the emergence of an anti-rabbinic sect in the ninth century. The Karaites themselves trace their origin to the split between the Northern and Southern Kingdoms after the death of King Solomon in the tenth century BCE. They maintain that Zadok the Priest had preserved the truth and handed it down through his descendants the Sadducees. The rediscovery of this truth was achieved by one Anan ben David in the 760s CE. The rabbinate version of the founding of Karaism is less romantic. They maintain that Anan ben David had been passed over as Exilarch and in retaliation had set up an alternative movement.

Anan's fundamental principle was expressed as 'search thoroughly in the Torah and do not rely on my opinion'. He insisted that the whole law was to be found in the biblical record and not in the rabbis' oral interpretations; Jewish observance must conform to biblical legislation rather than rabbinical ordinances. This does not mean that Anan made the yoke of the law easier to bear. In fact he made it harder: he did not recognize the minimum quantities of forbidden food accepted by the rabbis; he was more severe in his definition of forbidden Sabbath work; he introduced more complicated regulations for the circumcision ceremony; he increased the number of fast days; and he was particularly strict in his interpretation of ritual cleanliness. In addition, he seems to have absorbed many elements of an older extra-talmudic tradition and he took over several doctrines from local Islamic sects. Apparently, for example, he believed in the transmigration of souls.

After his death there was no clear leader and the movement split up into innumerable small groups and sects. The strict followers of Anan called themselves Ananites, and lived mainly in Egypt. Other sects opposed much of Anan's teaching, but were united in their opposition to the rabbis. As one of the early leaders put it, 'The rabbis believe that their laws and regulations were transmitted by the prophets; if that were the case, there ought not to exist any differences of opinion among them . . . We, on the other hand, arrive at our views by our reason, and reason can lead to various results.' However, by the late ninth century, a consensus had emerged. Its central representative was Benjamin ben Moses Nahavendi, who was the first to use the term 'Karaite'. He emphasized the free independent individual study of Scripture as the source of ethical guidance. By the tenth century, Karaite communities were established in Egypt, North Africa, Babylonia, Persia and Israel. There was a concerted attempt to spread Karaite ideas throughout the Jewish community, although this was resisted by such prominent Rabbanites as Saadiah Gaon.

Initially, Karaite scholars flourished in the Islamic empire. There were outstanding theologians, grammarians, lexicographers and biblical exegetes. Their contribution to biblical scholarship was particularly strong and includes the translation of the Hebrew Scriptures into Arabic with full commentary by Japheth ben Ali in the late tenth century. Israel became a centre for Karaite theology until the late eleventh century when members of both the Karaite and the Rabbanite communities were driven into a synagogue in Jerusalem by Christian crusaders and burnt alive. Activity continued for a time in Egypt, but soon the Karaite centre shifted to the Byzantine empire. From there communities were founded in the Crimea, Poland and Lithuania. By the fifteenth century some sort of rapprochement had been established between Karaite and Rabbanite scholars, but by the late sixteenth century Karaism was in severe decline.

Traditionally, Karaites were always treated as Jews by their host nations. At the end of the eighteenth century, however, when the Russians invaded the Crimea, a distinction was made. Karaites were relieved of the double taxation payable by the Jews and were allowed to purchase land. Later they were exempt from military service and were designated not as 'Jew-Karaites', but as 'Russian Karaites of the Old Testament faith'. By 1932 there were estimated to be about 10,000 Karaites in Russia and perhaps 2,000 elsewhere in Europe. They were spared by the Nazis in the Holocaust on the grounds that they were not of Jewish stock.

After the creation of the State of Israel, the remaining communities in Arab countries were subject to persecution and as many as 7,000 have now settled in Israel. There they have their own slaughterers, circumcisers and bet din (court) to administer their marriage and divorce laws. They are not permitted either by their own laws or by the laws of Israel to intermarry with the Jewish population.

4. THE GOLDEN AGE OF SPANISH JEWRY

The Islamic empire began to show signs of disintegration as early as the eighth century. In 750 the Abbasid Caliphs conquered the Ummayads, while Spain remained independent under an Ummayad leader. The Abbasid caliphate was less than stable; outlying territories were lost and after 850, the Caliph became essentially a figurehead for Turkish army rule. In 909, Shí'ite Muslims, who were followers of the Prophet

Muhammad's son-in-law 'Alí, took control of North Africa; known as the Fatamids, by 969 they had conquered Egypt and Israel. By the end of the tenth century, the once unified Islamic world had been fragmented into a number of different provinces, the rulers of which did not always coexist harmoniously.

This fragmentation of the Muslim empire was accompanied by a decentralization of the Jewish establishment. The two great academies of Sura and Pumbedita had moved to Baghdad, but this did not stem the decline in their prestige. Alternative academies (yeshivot) were established throughout the Jewish world. There the Talmud was studied, and the status of each yeshivah depended on the reputation of its individual teachers. Particularly prominent were the yeshivot of Israel. In Tiberias and later at Ramleh, Masorete scholars such as Asher ben Asher edited the Hebrew text of the Bible by devising a system of vowels and punctuation. Jewish life also flourished in Egypt, and yeshivot were established in Cairo and Kairouan. Also in North Africa, the Moroccan city of Fez was a prominent centre of rabbinic learning. There one of the most important scholars of the eleventh century, Isaac Alfasi, compiled an important code of Jewish law.

Spain was the scene of perhaps the greatest blossoming of Jewish culture. Southern Spain continued to be ruled over by the Ummayads in the tenth century. The Caliphs Abd Al-Rahman III (921–961) and Hakam II (961–972) employed Hasdai ibn Shaprut as their court physician. He was highly influential in the capital city of Cordoba. He acted as head of the Jewish community and was a noted patron of Jewish scholarship, and was also a diplomat, negotiating on behalf of the Caliph with the Christian rulers of the north. He is the first of several examples of Jewish statesmen in mediaeval Spain. Cordoba lost its prominence with the decline of the Ummayad dynasty in the eleventh century, but Jews also achieved success in the other provinces. Samuel ha-Nagid was vizier and army commander in the State of Granada between 1030 and 1056. Seville had several prominent Jewish courtiers. Lucena had an important yeshivah led by Isaac Alfasi, and Saragossa was the home of the poet and philosopher Solomon ibn Gabirol. Other important communities included Denia, Tudela, Almeria and Huesca. Toledo even had a significant Karaite as well as a prosperous Rabbanite community.

In 1146, the Almohads, a fanatical Moroccan dynasty, began their conquest of Muslim Spain and the situation rapidly changed for the worse. The practice of the Jewish religion was forbidden, yeshivot and synagogues were closed down and Jews were compelled to convert to Islam. Many fled north to the Christian area of Spain; others who did convert continued to observe Jewish practices in secret. Meanwhile in the Christian provinces from the tenth century, the Jews were generally seen as an important sector of the population. As the Christian kings expanded their territories at the expense of their Muslim neighbours, Jews were encouraged to settle and were, to a large extent, protected. According to legend, the Spanish hero El Cid employed Jews in his entourage and King Alfonso VI made use of Jewish expertise in medicine, finance and administration. It has been estimated that in Barcelona around one-third of the estates were in Jews' hands.

Although the rich land-owning Jews frequently had received an identical education to that of their Christian counterparts, the majority of Spanish Jewry continued to look to their traditional cultural heritage. The work of poets such as Judah Halevi, Moses ibn Ezra and Solomon ibn Gabirol is enshrined in the Jewish liturgy to this day. Biblical scholars such as Abraham ibn Ezra produced their commentaries and grammars in Hebrew and so influenced later generations of French and German scholars. The great philosopher Maimonides grew up in Spain although he was forced to flee to North Africa to escape the Almohads' persecution. Talmudic studies gained new impetus through the work of such as Nahmanides and Solomon ben Abraham Adret; both Maimonides and Jacob ben Asher produced important codes of Jewish law and the largest part of the great Jewish mystical work, the *Zohar*, was compiled by Moses ben Shem Tov de Leon between 1280 and 1286. It was a period of astonishing vitality and productivity.

5. JEWS IN CHRISTIAN EUROPE

Despite the extraordinary military success of the Islamic armies, much of Europe and the Byzantine empire remained Christian. The early Jewish communities of Western Europe were self-contained units. Their Christian overlords recognized no official Exilarch, so each community established its own rules and customs and administered its own bet din (court). By the tenth century there were important centres of Jewish learning in northern France, at Troyes and Sens, and in the

Rhineland, at Worms and Mainz. Eminent scholars included the halakhist (legal expert) Rabbenu Gershom of Mainz (960–1040) and the towering figure of Rashi (Solomon ben Isaac of Troyes, 1040–1105). Rashi and his school, the Tosafists, produced commentaries on all the books of the Bible and on all the orders of the Talmud. They made the text accessible not only to their contemporaries, but to generations of later students.

Jewish existence in Christian Europe was perilous. After Pope Urban II had proclaimed the First Crusade in 1096, Jews were attacked and massacred in several Rhineland towns. Increasingly the Jew was perceived as a demonic Christ-killer. Fuelling the religious suspicion of the Jewish outsider was a strong economic motive. The Christian guilds forced the Jews out of trade by their restrictive practices and the Jews turned to moneylending, which was forbidden by the Church to Christians. Then, not only was the Jew seen as a murderer, he was a cold-blooded usurer. As early as 1144, the Jewish community of Norwich was accused of using the blood of Christian children in the manufacture of Passover matzos (unleavened bread), and this blood libel spread throughout Europe. In addition the religious authorities became more involved in the 'Jewish problem'; for example the Fourth Lateran Council of the Church laid down that Jews should be immediately distinguishable from other people by their clothing.

Members of the Dominican order were particularly active against the community. In 1240 they held a debate in Paris with the leading Jewish scholars of the day during which the Dominicans were allowed the last word at each session, and afterwards the Talmud was publicly condemned and burnt. Later, in Barcelona in 1263, a disputation was held between the great scholar Nahmanides and a Jewish apostate known as Pablo Christiani. Although the King of Aragon gave Nahmanides three hundred gold coins, the secular government turned against the Jews, and as debts to Jewish moneylenders piled up, the rulers of Christian Europe saw the expulsion of the Jews from their domains as the answer to their economic difficulties. In 1182, the King of France expelled all Jews who lived on the royal estates, and cancelled all Christian debts to Jewish creditors. In 1290 the entire Jewish community was expelled from England where they had lived since the time of William the Conqueror, and the French king followed the English example a few years later. At about the same time, Jews in Germany were suffering violent attacks and in 1298, mobs destroyed approximately 150 communities. In the next century, when the Black Death raged through Europe the Jews were widely blamed; they were said to practise sorcery and to poison the wells. In the fourteenth and fifteenth centuries, massacre and expulsion became a frequent part of the Jewish experience. The great exception was Poland, where Jews were protected from the thirteenth century. Here Jews became tax collectors, fiscal agents and managers of the great nobles' estates.

Initially the Jewish community of Christian Spain had enjoyed a similar measure of security. At the end of the fourteenth century, however, political instability led to the persecution of the communities of Castile and Aragon and in 1413, a public disputation between Jews and Christians was held at Tortosa. Twenty-two rabbis including Joseph Albo spoke, and it extended to sixty-nine sessions.

Nonetheless there was increased pressure on the Jewish community to accept baptism and many Jews did become apostates. Possibly because there had been a degree of assimilation in Spain and the Jewish 'nobility' had experienced the same aristocratic education as their Christian counterparts, conversion to Christianity was not regarded with such horror as it was in the communities of Northern Europe. In any case these Conversos or Marranos, as they were called, found life much easier and many initially achieved social acceptance and high positions in the Church and the government. As time went by, however, the Conversos began to be regarded with suspicion. It was thought that they continued to follow Jewish practices in secret. When in 1480 King Ferdinand and Queen Isabella brought the Inquisition to Spain, thousands of Conversos were convicted and many were burnt at the stake for heresy. Those who had remained faithful to their heritage were not spared, although the Inquisition only had jurisdiction over those who were at least nominally Christian. The Jews were expelled from Spanish soil in 1492, and thus the great Jewish community of the Iberian peninsula was scattered; some went to North Africa, some to Italy, others to Holland and to Turkey.

SUGGESTED FURTHER READING

I. Abrahams, *Jewish Life in the Middle Ages*, Athenaeum, 1969.

J. Katz, *Tradition and Crisis: Jewish Society at the End of the Middle Ages*, Jewish Publication Society, 1950.

J.R. Marcus, ed., *The Jew in the Medieval World*, Harper and Row, 1965.

E. Schürer, *The History of the Jewish People in the Age of Jesus*, T. and T. Clark, 1973.

7 THE JEWISH PHILOSOPHICAL TRADITION

1. RABBINIC THEOLOGY

The rabbis of the talmudic period were not speculative philosophers or theologians, but it is possible to reconstruct their ideas from their midrashim (biblical commentaries) and from the aggadic (non-legal) sections of the Talmud. They expressed their beliefs in stories, legends, moral maxims and parables. Often their teaching originated in sermons given in the synagogues and this teaching was intended to be a guide to the problem of everyday living.

God's unity was seen to be of supreme importance. God is known by many different names in the Hebrew Bible, but the rabbis insist that He is always the same. He is the sole source of the universe and He directs it according to His own inscrutable plan. As Rabbi Abba bar Memel puts it, 'God said to Moses: "Thou desirest to know my name. I am called according to my deeds. When I judge my creation, I am called Elohim; when I wage war against the wicked, I am called Sabbaoth; when I suspend judgment for a man's sin, I am called El Shaddai; but when I have compassion on my world, I am called YHWH."' Thus idolatry is soundly and vigorously condemned: 'He who commits idolatry denies the Ten Commandments, and all that was commanded to Moses, to the Prophets and to the Patriarchs. He who renounces idolatry, it is as if he has professed the whole law.'

For the Tannaim and the Amoraim, God is the supreme transcendent Creator of the universe. Yet He is also intimately concerned with human affairs. As the Talmud puts it, 'God is far and yet He is near . . . For a man enters a synagogue and stands behind a pillar and prays in a whisper, and God hears his prayer, and so it is with all His creatures. Can there be a nearer God than this? He is as near to His creatures as the ear is near to the mouth.' Despite God's love and compassion for all of humanity, the rabbis believed that the Jewish people had a special role in the divine plan. A midrash on the verse 'I am the Lord who brought you up out of the Land of Egypt, to be your God. You shall therefore be Holy as I am Holy' (Leviticus 11:45) states: 'This means that God brought the Israelites out of Egypt on the condition that they would receive the yoke of the Commandments.' And it is emphasized that God's concern was profoundly loving: 'Like a king who entrusted his son to a tutor and then kept asking him, "Does my son eat; does he drink; has he gone to school; has he come back from school?", so God yearns to make mention of the Israelites at every hour.'

Some rabbinic writings describe the Torah as pre-existent and the instrument by which the universe was created. One midrash on Genesis explains, 'God created the world by His Torah; the Torah was His handmaid and His tool by the aid of which He set bounds to the deep, assigned the functions to the sun and the moon and formed all nature.' The Torah is the Word of God. Every word, every letter is sacred and its study is the Jews' most precious privilege. As Rabbi Ben Bag Bag suggests, the pious Jew 'will turn it and turn it over again, for everything is in it; contemplate it and wax grey and old over it, and stir not from it for you can have no better rule than this.' It was thought that there was layer upon layer of meaning in the text of the Torah and a lifetime was a less than adequate period for its study.

The rabbis also wrestled with such problems as the reconciliation of God's omniscience with the reality of human free will, with the question of human destiny and the afterlife and with the problem of the compatibility of God's justice with His mercy. Unlike their halakhic rulings, these theological speculations were not considered binding on the Jewish community. They were intended to inspire, educate and comfort those to whom they were spoken. They gave an underpinning for further teaching on such topics as martyrdom, repentance, forgiveness, atonement and charity. The study of the Torah, for the sages, was both the ultimate duty and the supreme pleasure; in a very real sense it was a fulfilment of the will of God.

2. SAADIAH GAON

In the first century CE, the Alexandrian philosopher Philo had tried to integrate Greek philosophy and Jewish teaching into a unified whole. He applied an allegorical method of interpretation to Scripture and he explained the God of Judaism in Greek philosophical terms (see Chapter 6, Part 1). Philo, who had himself been influenced by the Greek Stoics, was the forerunner of mediaeval Jewish philosophy, which also tried to reconcile fundamental Jewish concepts with the alternative philosophical systems of the day. The Jewish philosophers of the Middle Ages were particularly influenced by the Islamic Kalam schools of the eighth to eleventh centuries.

The beginnings of this philosophical development were in Babylon in the ninth century, when the rabbinic tradition was under threat from within by Karaite scholars (see Chapter 6, Part 3). The Karaites maintained that the view of God in talmudic and midrashic sources was all too frequently anthropomorphic. Meanwhile Muslim theologians were arguing that God's revelation to Moses on Mount Sinai (as well as in the Christian Gospel) was now superseded by the words of God as recorded by Muhammad in the Qur'án. The Zoroastrians and the Manichaeans, on the other hand, were attacking the whole concept of monotheism and questioning whether it could be the foundation of a viable religious system. In addition, other philosophers were maintaining that the Hellenistic philosophical world-view could account for the existence of the universe and that there was no need to bring in a divine being at all.

The great Jewish philosopher of the tenth century, Saadiah ben Joseph al Fayyumi (882–942) attempted to confront these questions. Born in Egypt, he finally settled in Babylon and became Gaon of the academy at Sura in 928–930 and 936–942. He was a prolific writer and was an expert in many fields. His *Siddur* ('Prayer Book') included Arabic rubrics and was one of the earliest systematic presentations of the Jewish liturgy. He translated the Hebrew Scriptures into Arabic and composed Arabic commentaries on many of the biblical books. He was also a poet, and his religious verse influenced a whole school of later piyyutim (poetry). He was an indefatigable opponent of the Karaites and his *Emunot ve-Deot* ('Book of Beliefs and Opinions') is generally regarded as the first great Jewish philosophical classic. In it the influence of Muslim Kalam philosophy can clearly be seen, in particular in his insistence that there is no contradiction between the findings of reason and the knowledge that comes from revealed religion.

Saadiah argued that the universe must have had a starting point. Against the Hellenistic philosophers, he asserted that time could not have evolved out of indefinite timelessness and that God, the Creator, is a single being who made the world out of nothing. Against the Zoroastrians, he insisted that although the Creator must have many attributes such as omnipotence and omniscience, these do not imply that God is a plurality. He responded to the Karaite criticism of anthropomorphism by pointing out that we are compelled to speak of God in human terms (such as talking of His eyes, His head or His hands) because of the inadequacy of human language, but he insisted that these descriptions were never intended to be taken literally.

Saadiah taught that human beings are composed of both bodies and souls. The soul is not pre-existent; it is created at the same time as the body and uses the body to act out its desires. God's commandments were given both to facilitate human communal life and as a mode of self-discipline. Obeying the laws has beneficial consequences in that the commandments enable human beings to live happily together and promote personal humility, charity and self-control. Ultimately humanity will be rewarded for its faithfulness. Saadiah accepted that many of the laws (such as those of ritual purity) have no rational justification and can only be explained as being the result of religious revelation.

Against the Muslims, he taught that the entire corpus of Jewish law, oral as well as written, was valid for all time. Individuals have free will to choose or to discard the good even though God's foreknowledge means that He knows in advance what the free human choice is going to be. It is in the afterlife that God both rewards those who have been faithful to Him and punishes the wicked.

Saadiah's definition of God and His attributes influenced generations of philosophers who came after him, and the *Emunot ve-Deot* laid the groundwork for all subsequent Jewish philosophical thinking.

3. THE JEWISH PHILOSOPHERS OF MEDIAEVAL SPAIN

Saadiah Gaon had been influenced by the Muslim Kalam philosophers, who had argued that there are four sources of reliable knowledge, namely the experience of the senses, the intuition of self-evident truths, logical reasoning and reliable tradition. From the eleventh century however, many Muslim thinkers had turned away from the Kalam school and were trying instead to find a rational basis for an unquestioning acceptance of the tradition. For example, they taught that everything that occurs in time and space occurs because it is God's will. This return to fundamentalist values was not appealing to the majority of Jewish philosophers, who increasingly came under the influence of neo-Platonic systems and those of the Aristotelians rather than their Muslim contemporaries.

The earliest Spanish philosopher to produce work in the neo-Platonic tradition was Solomon ben Joseph ibn Gabirol (c. 1022–1070). Little is known of his life, but besides his philosophical work he was also a notable poet. His secular verse describes both everyday joys and acute personal sorrows; much of his religious poetry has been incorporated into the religious liturgy (see Chapter 6, Part 4). His chief philosophical work was the *Fountain of Life*, which has only survived in a Latin translation. In it he argued that human beings are microcosms incorporating within themselves not only the material, but also the intelligible world. He taught that our physical world issued forth from the spiritual Creator at the end of a long chain of emanations, and that the universe consists of cosmic existences all flowing out from the light of the one God and, to some extent, all reflecting His glory. This idea of emanation was later to be very influential on the thinking of the great Jewish mystics (see Chapter 8).

Another philosopher of the Golden Age of Spanish Jewry was Bahya ben Joseph ibn Pakuda (c.1050–1120), the author of the *Duties of the Heart*. This was an extremely popular ethical guide that warned against over-scrupulousness in the observance of the Jewish commandments (the duties of the limbs) at the expense of the inward duties (the duties of the heart). Like ibn Gabirol, Bahya insisted that the human soul is of divine origin, and the treatise attempts to lead the reader through various spiritual steps towards communion with God and ultimate perfection. The *Duties of the Heart* has been printed in many editions and is one of the best-known Jewish devotional books.

Another important philosophical book of the period was *Exalted Faith*, written by Abraham ben David Halevi ibn Daud (c.1110–1180). Strongly influenced by Aristotelianism, ibn Daud argued that God's absolute unity could be deduced from His necessary existence. He maintained that the ultimate goal of humanity was to achieve perfection of knowledge, and this ideal could be identified with the acquisition of faith. Ibn Daud is also remembered as an historian and his *Book of Tradition* adds a great deal to our knowledge of Spanish Jewry.

Perhaps the best-known Jewish thinker of this era was Judah Halevi (1075–1141). His *Kuzari* ('The Book of the Khazars') draws on the legendary conversion to Judaism of the king of the Khazar tribe (see Chapter 6, Part 2). It consists of a dialogue between the king and a Jewish rabbi. The rabbi defends Judaism against the teachings of Christianity, Islam and Aristotelian philosophy. Using the classical philosophical form, the Platonic dialogue, Halevi argued that divine revelation and not rational thinking was the ultimate source of religious belief. He pointed out that the God who is defined as First Cause or Underlying Principle cannot be concerned with the activities of human beings. God encounters His people through revelation, and only in the pages of the Torah can the true God be found. Despite this critique of reason, Halevi insisted that Judaism was not opposed to science – he himself was a physician by profession and he believed that science had first originated among the Jews. Study of the Torah, he believed, does not conflict with the study of the world of nature. Nonetheless, Halevi was well aware of the inadequacy of the unaided rational faculty in determining religious truths, and in the *Kuzari* he offered an important challenge to the Aristotelian rationalism in the philosophy of his day.

4. MOSES MAIMONIDES AND THE MAIMONIDEAN CONTROVERSY

Arguably the leading intellectual figure of mediaeval Jewry was Rabbi Moses ben Maimon (1135–1204), known as Maimonides or Rambam. He made a major contribution to both the halakhic and the philosophical traditions. His great legal code, the *Mishneh Torah* ('Second Law') is an extraordinary synthesis of Jewish law organized within a clear logical framework. Comprehensive in scope, it covered the entire gamut of rabbinic law including regulations no longer operative, such as those concerned with Temple ritual. Included within the code was a discussion on the fundamentals of the Jewish religion, and it dealt with such subjects as the nature of God, the divine attributes, religious language and the foundation of ethics. Maimonides' major philosophical work, *Dalilat al-Hariain* ('Guide to the Perplexed') set the tone for all subsequent philosophical debate. Originally composed in Arabic, the Guide was an attempt to reconcile contradictions between Aristotelian philosophy and the traditional teachings of the rabbis.

Maimonides was born in Cordoba, Spain, but as a young man was compelled to flee Spain and settle in North Africa as a result of the accession of the fanatical Almohad dynasty (see Chapter 6, Part 4). Trained as a physician, he became head of the Jewish community of Fostat in 1177 and was appointed Court Physician to Saladin's Vizier in 1185. He was thus in an admirable position to understand the theological perplexities of his educated fellow countrymen.

Maimonides argued that the anthropomorphic language used to describe God in the Hebrew Scriptures was not intended to be understood literally, but metaphorically – God is not a corporeal being, and physical attributes referred not to Himself, but to His activities. Having discussed the philosophical proofs for the existence of God, he turned his attention to prophecy, which he said was an inspiration from God that required both the active intellect and a perfect development of the imagination. Moses was the greatest of the prophets, unique in that he prophesied continually and was able to hand down legislation that both regulated society and provided for individual spiritual well-being and perfection. Later Maimonides examined the nature of good and evil; he explained the doctrine of divine providence and concluded with his interpretation of the commandments and with a picture of the ideal human being. As he put it: 'Let not the wise man glory in his wisdom, let not the mighty man glory in his might, let not the rich man glory in his riches; but let him who glories glory in this, that he understands and knows . . . the Lord who practises steadfast love, justice and right-eousness in the earth.'

Maimonides' philosophy not only influenced later Jewish writers, it also had an impact on eminent Christian scholars such as Albertas Magnus and St Thomas Aquinas. Within the Jewish community it was the focus for a series of controversies both during the philosopher's lifetime and afterwards. Maimonides' attempt to synthesize the rabbinic tradition with classical philosophy was generally welcomed by members of the upper stratum of Jewish society; others were horrified. Earlier Judah Halevi had warned: 'Let not Greek wisdom tempt you, for it bears flowers only and no fruit.' The great halakhists and commentators of northern France anathematized Maimonides' works. The Spanish scholar Nahmanides (1197–1270) tried to defend the Guide on the grounds that upper-class Spanish Jews were so assimilated that if it were not for the writings of Maimonides, they would have been lost to Judaism altogether. There was a flurry of letters, sermons, accusations and counter-accusations. However, the participants in the controversy drew back aghast when Maimonides' books were publicly burnt by the Dominicans in 1232, and when his tomb in Tiberias was desecrated by his detractors.

The confrontation between the rationalists and the anti-rationalists was revived at the end of the thirteenth century. Solomon ben Abraham Adret of Barcelona condemned anyone under the age of twenty-five who studied Greek metaphysics, but this was strongly opposed by several authorities in Spain and Provence. The tension continued throughout the Middle Ages. On the one hand rationality was justified as being of the very essence of Judaism, but on the other it was condemned as a cause for apostasy and the reason for the Conversos' readiness to abandon their own tradition and embrace Christianity.

5. LATER JEWISH PHILOSOPHY

The masterpieces of mediaeval Jewish philosophy – Saadiah Gaon's *Emunot ve-Deot*, Judah Halevi's *Kuzari* and Moses Maimonides' *Dalilat al-Hariain* – had all been translated into Hebrew by the mid-thirteenth century and were therefore accessible to the scholars of France, Germany, Provence and Italy. In addition, the writings of Plato and Aristotle (previously only known in Averroes' Arabic version) were also made available.

The most prominent Jewish scholar after Maimonides was Levi ben Gershom, known as Gersonides (1288–1344). A native of Provence, he also was attracted to Aristotelianism and was an authority on law, mathematics and astronomy as well as philosophy. His major theological work was the *Wars of the Lord*, in which he discussed such matters as the creation of the world, divine providence, miracles, the nature of the soul and the phenomenon of prophecy. In several areas he differed from Maimonides and he went much farther in interpreting traditional Jewish doctrines in the light of Aristotelianism. For example, unlike Maimonides, he taught that the world was created from eternal matter, not out of nothing, and that God's providence was concerned with universals and not with the individual fate of human beings. Gersonides was among the last of the Jewish Aristotelians and was sharply criticized by his successors.

The last major philosopher of Spanish Jewry was Hasdai Crescas (1340–1412) of Barcelona. Crescas composed his book, *The Light of the Lord*, in Saragossa. In it he attempted to refute Aristotelianism and to distance himself from the thought of Maimonides and Gersonides by criticizing the traditional proofs for the existence of God. He called into question the concept of the Unmoved Mover, and argued that there may be an infinite void outside the universe, and that there might be many worlds. He insisted that the only certain base was the authority of the Scriptures and that love of God, not intellectual understanding, was the cornerstone of Judaism.

After Crescas the philosophical approach to religion lost its appeal, and writers became more concerned with defining the fundamental doctrines of Judaism. In this, Maimonides had already led the way. In his commentary on the Mishnah, he outlined thirteen principles of the Jewish faith:

> The existence of God
> His unity
> His incorporeality
> His eternity
> That prayer can be addressed to Him alone
> That the prophets are true
> That Moses is the supreme prophet
> That God gave the Torah to Moses
> That the Torah is immutable
> That God is omniscient
> Eventual reward and punishment
> The coming of the Messiah
> The resurrection of the dead.

These thirteen principles had been criticized by Hasdai Crescas, who proposed an alternative list of eight. Later Spanish thinkers, such as Simon ben Zemah Duran (1361–1444), Joseph Albo (1380–1445), and Isaac Arama (1420–1494) largely devoted their writings to critiques of Maimonides' formulation. Another philosopher, Isaac Abravanel (1437–1508) felt the whole attempt to isolate the fundamental principles of Judaism was misguided, because it implied that some parts of the Torah are more significant than others, whereas the Torah by its very nature is divinely inspired throughout.

By the end of the fifteenth century, the use of Greek philosophy as a weapon to defend the Jewish religion from internal and external assaults had largely ceased. Increasingly, succeeding generations turned their attention to the mystical tradition (see Chapter 8) as a basis for speculation about the nature of God and His relationship with His creation. In general, Jewish philosophy from the time of Philo had developed as the result of contact with the secular philosophies of the time; Philo had been influenced by Stoicism, Saadiah Gaon by the Muslim Kalam school, Solomon ibn Gabirol by the neo-Platonists and Maimonides by Aristotelianism.

Later, in the seventeenth century, Baruch Spinoza was to be similarly influenced by Descartes, but his philosophy led him away from traditional Judaism. Spinoza was to be rejected by his own people and his place is in the general history of western thought rather than in specifically Jewish philosophy. It was only in the late eighteenth century, with the Enlightenment and the breaking down of ghetto walls, that Jewish thinkers again began to make use of secular philosophy to explain and justify their religious beliefs – this will be discussed in a later chapter.

SUGGESTED FURTHER READING

J.L. Blau, *The Story of Jewish Philosophy*, Random House, 1962.
L. Jacobs, *A Jewish Theology*, Darton, Longman and Todd, 1973.
S. Katz, ed., *Jewish Philosophers*, Jewish Publishing Company, 1975.
S. Schechter, *Aspects of Rabbinic Theology*, Shocken, 1961.

8 MYSTICISM

1. EARLY RABBINIC MYSTICISM

Within the great treasury of the Talmud and in the midrashic literature, there are hints of mystical speculation. Often the mystical doctrines were kept secret. In a midrash on the book of Genesis, for example, it was reported that the custom was to repeat these hidden traditions in a whisper, so that they would not be overheard by the unlearned. There is a story about Rabbi Simeon ben Jehozadak and Rabbi Samuel ben Nahman. When Rabbi Simeon asked how light was created, Rabbi Samuel responded in a whisper. Asked why, he replied, 'Just as I myself had it whispered to me, even so have I whispered it to you'. It was understood that this secret knowledge was restricted to a small group, and Rabbi Judah taught that the hidden name of God should only be imparted to a man who is 'modest and meek, in the mid-way of life, not easily provoked to anger, temperate and free from vengeful feelings'.

Various strands can be distinguished within this early tradition. First there is merkavah ('chariot') mysticism, connected with the first chapter of the book of Ezekiel, in which God's chariot is described. The aim of this contemplative system was to be a 'merkavah rider', to free oneself from the chains of physical existence and ascend to the realm of paradise. Some particularly saintly individuals were thought to be able to ascend temporarily to the divine realm and then return to earth to convey the deepest secrets of the heavens to others; these mystics followed strict ascetic regimes involving prayer, fasting and ablution. Their experiences were related in the hekhalot ('heavenly hall') literature, which dates from the time of the Gaonim (seventh to eleventh centuries).

Closely associated with merkavah mysticism were speculations about the process of Creation. The rabbis used to discuss the hidden meaning of the stories in the book of Genesis. One of the most important texts on the subject, which may date from as early as the second century CE, was the *Sefer Yetzirah* ('Book of Creation'). This taught that the universe was created from thirty-two paths, consisting of the ten sefirot (emanations of God) and the twenty-two letters of the Hebrew alphabet.

A whole system was devised for understanding the meaning of the alphabet. The letters were said to have been 'hewn, combined, weighed and interchanged' and were classified according to three different types – mothers, doubles and singles. The three mother letters, namely alef, mem and shin, stand respectively for the three elements, air, water and fire. In the microcosm of the human form they represent the chest (air), the belly (water) and the head (fire). The seven double letters are beth, gimel, daleth, caf, peh, resh and tau. These were said to have 'formed, designed, created and combined' into the seven stars in the sky, the seven days of the week and the seven orifices of human perception (two eyes, two ears, two nostrils and one mouth). Finally the twelve single letters correspond to the twelve chief human activities (sight, hearing, smell, speech, hunger, the sexual appetite, movement, anger, mirth, thought, sleep and work), to the twelve signs of the zodiac, to the twelve months of the year and to the twelve limbs of the body. Within the system human beings are seen as a reflection of the whole universe of space and time and everything within that universe derives from the activities of the Hebrew letters.

The ten sefirot supplement the doctrine of the Creation from the alphabet. The first of God's emanations is the Spirit of God; the second is the element air which derives from the Spirit. On the air the twenty-two letters were thought to be hewn. From air comes the water from which is derived the chaos and the darkness out of which the earth was formed. The fourth emanation is the fire which derives from the water and from which God made the angelic hosts of Heaven and the merkavah. The last six sefirot are the spatial dimensions, north, south, east, west, height and depth.

The early mystics taught that God transcends His universe, yet everything came into existence out of His emanations. God is imminent in His universe through His sefirot, therefore, but in Himself He is utterly transcendent. This cosmic speculation proved to be the foundation for much later mystical speculation throughout the Middle Ages.

2. THE HASIDEI ASHKENAZ

The early mystical texts were particularly studied in the Rhineland from the ninth century onwards. The eleventh and twelfth centuries were the period of the Crusades.

Rumours were circulating in Western Europe that a 'Prince of Babylon' had destroyed the Holy Sepulchre in Jerusalem and was also encouraged by the Jews to kill Christians. The Pope declared the First Crusade, and many Christian townspeople took it upon themselves to attack their Jewish neighbours. The first massacre took place in Speyer in 1096, another occurred in Worms and a third at Mainz. So terrifying was the slaughter that adult Jews killed their own children rather than let them fall into the hands of their Christian neighbours. The bishops and noblemen made some attempt to save the Jews under their protection, but thousands of Jewish lives were lost.

There was another anti-Semitic outburst in 1146, when Pope Eugenius III and St Bernard of Clairvaux preached a new Crusade, and later in the twelfth century the Third Crusade led to further massacres. The Hasidei Ashkenaz ('pious men of Germany') must be understood against this background. They did not make up an organized movement, but consisted of several groups of scholars who flourished independently of each other in the late twelfth and early thirteenth centuries. In the German school, mystical ideas had been discussed secretly for several generations. Study was based on the *Sefer Yetzirah* and on the texts of merkavah and hekhalot mysticism (see Part 1). It was also claimed that secrets had been inherited from the Babylonian schools and had been preserved in certain families down the centuries.

One of the earliest writers of the Hasidei Ashkenaz was Rabbi Judah ben Samuel he-Hasid ('the Pious'), who was writing in the mid-twelfth century. His most important work was the *Sefer Hasidim* ('Book of the Pious'), a detailed volume of ethics. It provides religious guidance on worship, prayer, study, education, dealings with non-Jews and social and family relationships. Rabbi Judah emphasized the paramount importance of spiritual effort; the more effort is required to keep a commandment or perform a righteous deed, the more meritorious it becomes. Sin must be atoned for by self-inflicted suffering, and every virtuous act necessarily involves a certain degree of hardship and sacrifice. The ultimate good deed, therefore, is Kiddush ha-Shem (martyrdom in the name of God). Giving up one's life for God is the supreme ethical achievement. Through his teaching Rabbi Judah helped to prepare his fellow Jews for the trials of Christian persecution, and he gave them some consolation for the nightmare that threatened them at that period.

Other books that emerged from the Hasidei Ashkenaz include the anonymous *Sefer ha-Hayyim* ('Book of Life'), and Rabbi Elhanan ben Yaher's *Sefer ha-Navon* ('Book of Navon') and *Sod ha-Sodot* ('Secret of Secrets'). In addition, Rabbi Eliezar of Worms, together with Rabbi Judah he-Hasid, wrote detailed commentaries on the Prayer Book. In general, the Hasidei Ashkenaz were opposed to philosophical enquiry, although they knew and used Saadiah Gaon's *Emunot ve-Deot* (see Chapter 7, Part 2). In their writings they were preoccupied with the mystery of God. They maintained that God Himself can never be known, and only His glory can be perceived; this had been revealed by the prophets and a vision of it can be attained through a life of devotion, discipline, piety and contemplation. To be a hasid (pious man) was the ideal, and was far more important than any intellectual achievement.

Another feature of the movement was an interest in magic. Eliezar of Worms wrote tracts on magic based on God's secret name. Techniques of mystical speculation were also taught, based on the numerical value of the letters making up a prayer or benediction. According to the system known as gematria, each Hebrew letter has a numerical value and the total value of particular words and prayers could be calculated to match them with alternative biblical passages or with the names of God. Prayer was understood as mystical ascent to God, and hymns and prayers were composed that reflected the peace and ecstasy to be found in devotion to the Lord. Thus, through the terrible insecurities of the twelfth and thirteenth centuries, the scholars of the Hasidei Ashkenaz movement gave their followers a sense of purpose and consolation in the face of persecution. Death was not to be feared, because Kiddush ha-Shem was the highest honour. The glory of the God of Israel shone throughout the world for those who were privileged enough to see it.

3. THE EMERGENCE OF THE *ZOHAR*

Mystical speculation was producing important work at the same time in southern France. In twelfth-century Provence, the *Sefer ha-Bahir* ('Book of Bahir') put forward a different interpretation of the concept of the sefirot from that originally suggested in the *Sefer Yetzirah*. The new interpretation pictured the sefirot as the crowns or vessels that make up the structure of the divine realm. Similarly Isaac the Blind (1160–1235) described the sefirot as emanations of a hidden dimension of the Godhead. He referred to the divine infinite as Ein Sof ('the Infinite'), which contains within itself absolute perfection without plurality or distinction. Drawing on neo-Platonic ideas, he maintained that the first emanation from Ein Sof was divine thought, and that the other sefirot were all further emanations from this. The inhabitants of the material world were merely materializations of the sefirot at a lower degree of reality, and the purpose of mystical contemplation was to ascend the ladder of the sefirot to unite with divine thought. Contemporary with Isaac the Blind was another group also working in southern France called the Iyyun ('contemplation') circle. This group was also influenced by the neo-Platonists, and produced several brief mystical treatises.

After this initial phase, a school of Kabbalah ('received tradition') developed in Gerona, northern Spain. Basing his work on that of Isaac the Blind, Azriel ben Menahem, for example, taught in the early thirteenth century that the divine will rather than divine thought was the first emanation of Ein Sof. The best-known figure of the Gerona circle was Moses ben Nahman (Nahmanides) (1197–1270). Nahmanides had defended Maimonides' philosophical thinking (see Chapter 7, Part 4) and had taken part in the famous Jewish–Christian disputation at Barcelona (see Chapter 6, Part 5). His involvement in kabbalistic speculation, combined with his profound halakhic knowledge, persuaded many of his fellow Jews that mystical ideas were compatible with traditional rabbinic scholarship. In his commentary on the Torah, he referred to kabbalistic concepts to explain the biblical text. For example, in his discussion on the meaning and purpose of ritual sacrifice, he argued that through sacrifice 'blessing emanates to the highest powers'.

Meanwhile, different mystical schools were at work in other parts of Spain. Drawing both on the traditions of the Hasidei Ashkenaz and that of the Sufis of Islam, Abraham ben Samuel Abulafia (1240–1271) explained how the letters of the Hebrew alphabet could be combined to fulfil the human aspiration towards prophecy. Another Spanish kabbalist, Isaac ibn Latif (1220–1290) taught that the divine will was the source of all the emanations and that the Kabbalah revealed a higher form of truth than philosophy. Another thirteenth-century mystic, Isaac ha-Kohen, suggested that there were ten demonic emanations that paralleled the divine sefirot.

Most significant of all was the appearance of the *Zohar* ('Divine Splendour') at the end of the thirteenth century. This was to prove the most influential text of the Jewish mystical tradition. The major part of the *Zohar* was composed by Rabbi Moses de Leon (1250–1305) and drew on the teachings of the Gerona school. Its subject, however, was based in the time after the Bar Kokhba revolt, in the second century CE, and focused on Rabbi Simeon bar Yohai and his disciples (see Chapter 5, Part 1).

Written in Aramaic as a midrash on the Torah, it taught that the sefirot emanated from the Godhead like a flame. They were identified as the Supreme Crown, Wisdom, Intelligence, Greatness, Power, Beauty, Endurance, Majesty, Foundation and Kingdom. The first three constituted the intellectual realm of the divine; the second group of three reflected the moral quality of the Godhead; the next three were archetypes for the forces of nature; and the tenth sefirah was the channel between the divine and the material world. Frequently the sefirot were portrayed as a tree, or as ten concentric circles (the spheres) or as an archetypal man representing the totality of the divine energy. The Kabbalah was never intended merely as a theoretical system. The *Zohar* taught that human action had a real effect on the higher world – through serving God, the pious soul would not only achieve union with the divine, it would bring repair ('tikkun') to the disharmony of the world, which had been brought about by the sin of Adam.

During the fourteenth and fifteenth centuries, the teachings of the *Zohar* spread beyond Spain into Germany, Israel, Italy and Byzantium, and by the sixteenth century it had become an integral part of mainstream Jewish culture.

4. LURIANIC KABBALAH

By the fifteenth century, the Ottoman Turks had become a major world power. Many Jews settled in Ottoman territories, and their number was increased by communities of Spanish Jews fleeing the general expulsion of 1492. In the sixteenth century there were flourishing Jewish communities in many parts of the Empire; Jews rose to important positions within the Ottoman court and there were successful academies at Cairo, Istanbul and Salonica. By this time, there was an acknowledged distinction between Jews from Spain and the Islamic countries and those who came from northern France, Germany and Eastern Europe. The former were known as the Sephardim, the latter as the Ashkenazim. Each group had its own distinctive customs and its own special language (Ladino and Yiddish respectively). When the Sephardic halakhic authority Joseph Caro (1488–1575) published his monumental code of Jewish law, the *Shulhan Arukh* ('Prepared Table'), Moses Isserles (1525-1572) had to add a supplement, *Mappah* ('Tablecloth'), to make it acceptable to Ashkenazi communities.

While working on the *Shulhan Arukh*, Caro had emigrated to Safed in Israel. Safed had a Jewish population of over 10,000 and had become an important centre, particularly for kabbalistic scholarship. Messianic expectation was rife; religious poetry was composed about the advent of the Messiah, and the mystics of Safed participated in ascetic rites such as wearing sackcloth, fasting and publicly confessing their sins. A prominent example of such ascetics was one Abraham ha-Levy Beruchim who, roaming the streets calling passers-by to repentance, is said to have led his followers back to the synagogue, wrapped himself in a sack and commanded his audience to throw stones at him. During this period the teaching of such kabbalistic scholars as Moses Cordovero (1522–1570) and Isaac Luria (1534–1572) was much studied.

Isaac Luria in particular can be said to have transformed the Jewish mystical tradition. He had grown up in Egypt and had spent seven years in solitude meditating on the *Zohar*. Although he only lived in Safed for two years before his death, he passed on his teaching to a small group of followers who spread it throughout Sephardic Jewry. Luria believed that in order to form the universe, the Ein Sof had to shrink into Himself (a process known as zimzum) to provide an empty space in which Creation could occur. Thus Creation was not an outpouring positive act, rather it was an initial withdrawing, an exile of the divine, to make a vacuum. After zimzum, light flowed from the Godhead and took on the shape of the sefirot. Each sefirah was in the form of a vessel, but so strong was the pure light of the divine that the vessels shattered, bringing upheaval and disaster to the emerging sefirot.

Following the shevirat ha-kelim (breaking of the vessels), the universe was divided into the kingdom of evil and the kingdom of the divine light. Even evil, however, derived its power from the divine light. Sparks of light had been retained when the vessels were broken and they gave sustenance to the evil world. Thus, there was a constant struggle to overcome evil forces, which was achieved by a never-ending process of emanation. Human beings were the battleground for the conflict – the sefirot were portrayed as Adam Kadmon (primal man). The biblical Adam was originally intended to defeat the evil forces of his body by means of his light-filled soul, but in this he failed and his failure paralleled the breaking of the vessels. There was cosmic upheaval, and evil, instead of being defeated, grew stronger. Subsequently, the people of Israel were chosen to overcome the darkness of the world, and Luria taught that the history of the Jews was the story of the attempt to recapture the escaped divine sparks, to transform the earthly sphere and finally to unite it once more with the divine.

Luria and his disciples believed that they were living in the final days. Keeping the commandments of God was the only means of effecting tikkun (repair) – every good deed led to the rescue of a divine spark, while every evil action resulted in a further plunge into evil and chaos. Every human deed has cosmic significance, therefore, and Luria was convinced that very soon the long-promised Messiah would appear to bring a final end to the struggle (see Chapter 4, Part 2). By the end of the seventeenth century, such messianic expectations had become a central feature of Jewish life in the Ottoman Empire.

5. SHABBETAI ZEVI, THE MYSTICAL MESSIAH

Into this milieu of messianic expectation arrived the self-proclaimed Messiah, Shabbetai Zevi (1626–1676). Born in Smyrna and ordained at the age of eighteen, Shabbetai was a gifted scholar who devoted himself to the study of the *Zohar*. His charismatic personality attracted many followers. He had been born on Tishah b'Av (the ninth day of Av), the annual day of lamentation for the destruction of the Temple and the traditional birthday of the Messiah; this may have encouraged his delusions. The Jewish people were then going through a particularly traumatic period; the highly successful community of Poland/Lithuania had been devastated by the Cossack Chmielnicki massacres in 1648, and this had the effect of encouraging Jews everywhere to hope for the immediate advent of a messianic redeemer.

Throughout his life, Shabbetai suffered from violent mood changes – deep depression was followed by times of euphoric activity, with occasional periods of calm. The rabbis of Smyrna expelled him from the city as an evil influence in 1650–51 and for the next few years he wandered through Greece and Turkey, attracting scandal wherever he went. After visiting Jerusalem he went to Cairo, where in 1664 he married a survivor of the Chmielnicki massacres, whom he described as 'the bride of the Messiah'. The turning point of his career came when he encountered Rabbi Nathan Benjamin Levi (1644–1680) in Gaza. Nathan recognized Shabbetai as the long-awaited redeemer and he himself took on the role of the forerunner of the Messiah, the prophet Elijah (see Chapter 3, Part 3). He sent messages throughout the Jewish world declaring that the Ottoman Sultan would soon be deposed, that the Ten Lost Tribes would return from their exile (see Chapter 3, Part 4), and describing the present troubles as the 'birth pangs of the Messiah'.

Diaspora Jewry was in turmoil. Many leading rabbis accepted Shabbetai's claims, while others stood aloof. The date of the messianic redemption was set for 18 June 1666, and meanwhile penitential dirges were sung, prayers were said for 'our Lord and King Shabbetai Zevi', fast days were transformed into festivals and believers disposed of all their property in preparation for the coming salvation. Doubters were excommunicated and exiled, and everywhere there was a sense of frenzied excitement. In January 1666, Shabbetai sailed to Constantinople, the Ottoman capital, where he was immediately arrested by the Turkish authorities. The fortress of Gallipoli quickly became a messianic court, with pilgrims coming from all over the world to receive the messianic blessing and participate in mystical rituals and ascetic practices. One of the visitors was the Polish kabbalist Nehemiah ha-Kohen, who subsequently denounced him. Shabbetai was brought to the court of the Grand Vizier and given the choice of being put to death or converting to Islam. Shabbetai and his wife chose to become Muslims, and he finally died in exile in Albania in 1676.

Amazingly, this was not the end of the story. Many of his followers were disenchanted and returned to the Jewish fold, but others, including Nathan of Gaza, remained unshaken in their faith. Nathan insisted that Shabbetai's conversion was part of a battle with the forces of evil. By descending into the abyss, the Messiah was liberating sparks of divine light to effect tikkun. He had chosen a 'messianic exile' to bring Israel's exile more quickly to an end. Others argued that it had not been Shabbetai who had converted to Islam, but a phantom – Shabbetai the Messiah had ascended to Heaven.

In any event, Shabbetean beliefs persisted even among the learned; Jonathan Eybeschutz (1690–1763), for example, became Chief Rabbi of Altona, Wandsbeck and Hamburg, but was accused by his rival Jacob Emden (1697–1776) of being a secret Shabbetean. Others followed Shabbetai into Islam, forming the Dönmeh ('apostate') sect. They retained a separate Jewish life and opposed intermarriage with Muslims, while rejecting much of the Torah; a Dönmeh community existed in Istanbul until the mid-twentieth century.

Even more radical were the Frankists. Jacob Frank (1726–1791) was influenced by the Dönmeh and believed that not only was he a reincarnation of Shabbetai Zevi, but also the second person of the Trinity. After a debate with traditional Jews, Frank and his followers were baptized and the cult, which involved licentious orgies, spread from Poland to Bohemia and Germany. By 1850 however, apart from the Dönmeh, Shabbeteanism had almost completely died out.

SUGGESTED FURTHER READING

I. Abelson, *Jewish Mysticism*, Harmon Press, 1969.
J. Dan, *Jewish Mysticism and Jewish Ethics*, Washington University Press, 1986.
G. Sholem, *Kabbalah*, Quadrangle, 1974.
G. Sholem, *Sabbatai Sevi: the Mystical Messiah*, Princeton University Press, 1973.

9 THE HASIDIM AND THE MITNAGGDIM

1. JEWRY IN EASTERN EUROPE

Jews who traced their descent from ancestors who had settled in Christian north-west Europe in the Middle Ages were known as the Ashkenazim. From the ninth century CE, Ashkenaz was identified with Germany, and between 1050 and 1300 these 'German' communities dominated England, France (except Provence), Holland, Flanders, the German states, Switzerland and northern Italy. After the expulsions of the Middle Ages, the Jews fled eastwards to Germany, Austria and Poland.

The Ashkenazim used different liturgical rites from the communities of Spain, North Africa and the Orient. They composed liturgical hymns known as piyyutim, and selihot (penitential prayers). The invention of printing helped preserve the Ashkenazi rite, which became known as minhag Polin (the 'Polish custom') and still forms the basis for synagogue worship throughout the Ashkenazi world.

The Ashkenazim were known for their talmudic scholarship and for their strict adherence to Jewish law. Rashi's commentaries were particularly influential (see Chapter 6, Part 5) and the Hasidei Ashkenaz with their readiness for Kiddush ha-Shem ('martyrdom') set an exalted standard of piety (see Chapter 8, Part 2).

Initially the rulers of Poland and Lithuania provided a secure basis for communal existence. The Jews were frequently employed as land agents and tax collectors, acting as intermediaries between the nobility and the peasantry. Because talmudic study was promoted daily within the community, the Jews enjoyed a standard of literacy unknown among their Christian neighbours. They also benefited from a system of communal autonomy; between about 1550 and 1764, the Council of the Four Lands regulated Jewish life throughout Poland and Lithuania. Yiddish was the communal language and the rabbis ran their own battei dinim (religious law courts) and numerous yeshivot (talmudic academies).

By the beginning of the fifteenth century, the Polish community numbered between ten and fifteen thousand people, and within a hundred years it increased tenfold. Despite various forms of discrimination such as having to wear distinctive clothing, and occasional accusations of using Christian blood to make Passover matzos, the Jews of Poland and Lithuania flourished, and Eastern Europe became a great centre of Jewish scholarship. The yeshivot concentrated on the differentiation and reconciliation of rabbinical opinion in talmudic law. Commentaries were written on Joseph Caro's *Shulhan Arukh* (see Chapter 8, Part 4) and a complex civilization was developed with its own traditions, social institutions, customs and values.

Coming against such a background of growth and prosperity, the Chmielnicki massacres were particularly traumatic. In 1648, Bogdan Chmielnicki was elected leader of the Cossacks and led a rebellion against the Polish gentry. The Jews, as the administrators of the nobles' estates, took the brunt of the punishment, and thousands died amid scenes of cruelty and torture. It has been estimated that a quarter of the entire Jewish community died in the onslaught, and many more were sold as slaves in the markets of Istanbul. Chmielnicki appealed to his Russian allies, who invaded north-west Poland and the Ukraine. The Russians, who would not allow Jews to settle in their land, joined the Cossacks in their slaughter. Meanwhile the Swedes seized the opportunity and advanced into western Poland; the Polish partisans believed that these invaders were encouraged by the Jews and did not hesitate to take their revenge upon the Jewish population.

Even into the eighteenth century, Jewish life in Poland continued to be insecure. Approximately a third of the population lived in the countryside in small villages known as shtetlakh, where they were subject to repeated accusations, and in the 1730s and 1740s the Cossacks again invaded the Ukraine and robbed and murdered the Jewish inhabitants. The entire community of Uman, for example, was butchered in 1768.

The government laid heavy taxes on the communities, but continued to allow them a degree of autonomy. The Jews were deeply discouraged, however, not only by the persecutions, but also by the conversion of the self-proclaimed Messiah, Shabbetai Zevi, to Islam (see Chapter 8, Part 5). Talmudic scholarship and traditional rabbinic learning had failed them. The Jews of eighteenth-century Eastern Europe were beginning to look to a different type of Judaism.

2. THE RISE OF THE HASIDIC MOVEMENT

The founder of this new religious movement was Israel ben Eliezer (c. 1700–1760) known as the Baal Shem Tov ('Master of the Good Name'), or the Besht. There is little reliable documentation on his life, but it is thought he was born in the village of Okup in the Carpathian Mountains. His early career was as a miracle worker and healer, and he seemed to have earned his living as a shohet (religious slaughterer) or as a schoolmaster. At that time there were several mystical leaders, each with their own circle of followers and each conveying their own particular truth; the Besht does not seem to have been an outstandingly learned scholar, but his circle soon became prominent. His teachings have not been systematically preserved, but they were eventually collected and published in rabbinic Hebrew. Presumably they were originally delivered in Yiddish.

Many of his aphorisms imply that true devotion to God is to be valued more highly than traditional rabbinic scholarship. As he put it, 'What matters is not how many precepts you fulfil, but the spirit in which you fulfil them', and 'There is no room for God in one who is full of himself'. There are many legends of the Besht getting the better of his learned opponents. On one occasion, for example, he was asked what should be done in the event of forgetting to insert the new-moon blessing into the daily liturgy. The Besht replied that he did not know – since he would never forget it! He taught that the study of Torah should be an exercise of devekut (devotion) and every aspect of daily life, whether eating, drinking or going about one's business, should also be performed in a spirit of worship. Serving God should be an occasion for joy; he used to say, 'Serve God with gladness; a joyful person has an abundance of love for man and for all God's creatures'.

The disciples of the Besht believed that he had been specially chosen by God because he offered prayers with such intense dedication. It is said that in order to focus his mind he used to smoke a pipe, and he would make wild gestures both as an aid to concentration and as an expression of longing for God. He always used to point out that a drowning man is not ashamed to gesticulate wildly so that others would come and rescue him.

The followers of the Besht were known as the Hasidim ('Pious Ones'), and after his death in 1760 the movement spread throughout Poland and beyond. He had two children; little is known of the son, but his daughter was the mother of Baruch the Tsaddik ('Righteous Leader') of Medzibozh (1757–1810) and was the grandmother of the famous Nahman of Bratslav (1772–1811). However, it was mainly through its disciples that the movement achieved its extraordinary success. Jacob Joseph of Polonnoye (c. 1710–1772) was known as the first Hasidic author. His *Tolodot Ya'akov Yosef* preserved many of the Besht's maxims and glorified Hasidic leaders as the 'channels through which God's influence flows to the common people'.

The leader who succeeded the Besht was Dov Baer, the Maggid (preacher) of Mezhirech (1710–1772). There may have been a struggle for the succession between Jacob Joseph and Dov Baer, but in any event Dov Baer managed to surround himself with a learned circle of disciples and his teachings were preserved in a collection published by his follower Solomon of Lutsk in 1781. Among his disciples, who in their turn became Hasidic leaders, were Levi Yitshak of Berdichev (c. 1740–1810), Shneur Zalman of Lyady (1745–1813) and Elimelech of Lyzhansk (1717–1787).

Hasidic ideas spread rapidly. The verse from Genesis, 'A river flowed out of Eden to water the garden; it then divided to become four branches', (2:10) was thought to refer to the spread of Hasidism in Poland. Eden stood for the Besht; the river for Dov Baer; the garden for Elimelech of Lyzhansk; and the four branches for four of his prominent disciples. In the early days, leadership was passed from master to follower, but succession quickly became a matter of family descent and sons followed fathers. This led to rivalry so that, for example, when Mordecai of Chernobl died in 1837, each of his eight sons founded a Hasidic dynasty. By the beginning of the nineteenth century, probably about half of Eastern European Jewry had given their allegiance to this new movement.

3. HASIDIC BELIEFS AND PRACTICES

Although Hasidism provided a new approach to Judaism, it was in no sense a new philosophy since it was based on ideas from the Bible, the

Talmud and the mystical tradition. It was primarily a reaction to the dry intellectualism of much traditional talmudic study, and through the inspiration of the Hasidic leaders, simhah (rejoicing) and hitlahavut (enthusiasm) became part of the religious experience of ordinary people. Devekut (devotion) was all-important; God must be kept constantly in mind, and every thought and every action should be an expression of attachment to the Creator. The Hasidim believe that God is everywhere in the Universe – as it is expressed in the *Zohar*, 'no space is void of Him'. Thus every human activity is capable of sanctification, and it is possible to worship the Master of the Universe without ceasing.

Central to the philosophy of Hasidism is the doctrine of the Tsaddik, or righteous man. For the Hasidim, their Tsaddik is their spiritual ruler and mentor. It is sometimes suggested that the doctrine of the Tsaddik was a later development within the movement, but this is not the case; the Baal Shem Tov himself was regarded as a Tsaddik, and the tradition dates back to him. As Jacob Joseph indicated, the Tsaddik is the channel through whom God's grace flows to the faithful, and it is by close association with his Tsaddik that the individual Hasid draws near to God.

From the early days, the Tsaddik held court; even today he is regularly visited by his followers, who observe his behaviour as a pattern to be followed. There is a story, for example, of a visitor to the Maggid of Mezhirech who went to see the Tsaddik, not to learn about the Torah from him, but to see how he tied his shoes. By watching the Tsaddik, the disciple can learn how God can be worshipped in every detail of everyday life. The Tsaddik holds mass audiences, gives individual advice and is supported by the donations of the faithful. When the Tsaddik presides over a communal meal, his disciples are eager to consume any food or drink he has left, as this is believed to be conducive to spirituality.

Although Hasidic communities were decimated by the Holocaust in Europe (see Chapter 12, Part 2), Hasidic groups survive today, particularly in Israel and in the United States. Little about them has changed. The Tsaddik is now generally called by the Yiddish title 'Rebbe', although those living in Israel tend to call their leader Admor, which is a Hebrew acrostic for 'our Lord, our Teacher and our Rabbi'. The Rebbe still holds court and is visited by his disciples.

Members of Hasidic sects are readily visible by their dress; the men characteristically wear black hats, beards and side-curls, black suits, and white shirts with their ritual fringes visible. On the Sabbath they appear resplendent in black silk kaftans over trousers and shirts, with magnificent fur hats, known as streimels, on their heads. The women are dressed modestly with high-necked dresses that cover wrists and knees. Married women keep their heads covered at all times, often with a wig called a sheitel. Men and women marry young, and contraception is discouraged. In the Hasidic areas of big cities, it is commonplace to see large Hasidic families out walking on the Sabbath – six or eight children are not unusual. The Rebbes, their spiritual leaders, are the direct descendants of the Hasidic Tsaddikim of the late eighteenth and early nineteenth centuries. Among the best-known groups today are the Lubavich, the Satmar, the Vizhits, the Belz, the Bobover and the Gur Hasidim.

Initially there was considerable conflict between the Hasidim and the mainstream rabbinic leaders. The Hasidim adopted a new prayer rite, based on the Prayer Book of Isaac Luria; they modified the Ashkenazi liturgy to include Sephardic elements; and they used their own ritual slaughterers. In addition they have produced a vast literature, which includes miraculous tales of the Tsaddikim as well as collections of the different Tsaddiks' homilies, either in the synagogue or over meals. The Hasidim believe that their Rebbe is directly inspired by God when he speaks, and some Rebbes even compose their own melodies as music and dance are regarded as important means of uplifting the soul. Even today, with their emphasis on spirituality and joy, the Hasidim remain a powerful force within the Jewish tradition.

4. THE VILNA GAON AND THE MITNAGGDIM

The Hasidim did not carry all before them, however. In the final decades of the eighteenth century, supporters of time-honoured rabbinic Judaism mounted a determined campaign against the new movement. These traditionalists were scornfully described as Mitnaggdim ('Opponents') by their Hasidic adversaries because they fiercely opposed the innovations introduced by the Baal Shem Tov and his followers. In particular they feared that Hasidism would prove to be another heretical popular movement leading to the same disastrous results as Shabbetai Zevi's messianism or the Frankist licentiousness (see Chapter 8, Part 5). They disapproved of Hasidic deviations from the established Ashkenazi Prayer

Book and the introduction of Sephardic rituals, and they were appalled by the setting up of alternative shtiblakh (small houses of worship) separate from the main synagogues. They deplored the Hasidic neglect of Torah and Talmud study and their disregard of painstaking scholarship and, most emphatically, they rejected the veneration of the Tsaddikim.

Hasidism spread northwards throughout Poland until it reached Lithuania, which was a stronghold of rabbinic learning – the community of Vilna was renowned as the most learned in Eastern Europe. Led by the remarkable Elijah ben Solomon Zalman (1720–1797), the Vilna Gaon, traditionalists sought to combat the teachings of the new movement. Elijah himself had been regarded as a child prodigy. He is said to have given a learned sermon in the Great Synagogue of Vilna when he was just six years old, and by the time he was thirteen he was considered to be a master of talmudic and kabbalistic knowledge. After his marriage, he travelled round the Jewish world, and then he returned to Vilna at the age of twenty-five. Although he lived as a recluse on the outskirts of the town, his outstanding scholarship was recognized and he received a regular pension from communal funds. He is said to have slept only two hours every night; he saw no one and studied continually, wrapped in his tallis (prayer shawl). He used to say that it was better to pray at home, because in the synagogue it was impossible to escape envy and the hearing of idle talk. Then, when he was forty, he emerged from seclusion and admitted a small band of disciples, all of whom were distinguished talmudic scholars, to his inner circle.

The Vilna Gaon was determined to preserve the values of traditional Judaism. He used to say that only things acquired by hard labour and great struggle are of any value, and disapproved of the exuberance of the Hasidim, believing that it undermined stringent scholarship. Consequently, he refused even to meet with the Hasidic leaders Menahem Mendel of Vitebsk and Shneur Zalman of Lyady. He ceremoniously burnt Hasidic books and pronounced a decree of herem (excommunication) against members of Hasidic groups.

In general the communities of Lithuania supported Elijah, but so acrimonious did the conflict become that it was not unknown for parents to observe the traditional rites of mourning if one of their sons joined a Hasidic sect. The bitter struggle continued even after Elijah's death; on one occasion each side even took the unheard-of step of appealing to the Russian government against the other.

Elijah's influence was by no means entirely negative. At this time talmudic study had become intensely complicated and hair-splitting, and in the yeshivot (talmudic academies) of Eastern Europe, a rigorous method of scholarship known as pilpul was taught. This involved juxtaposing unrelated texts and artificially forcing them into a relationship; it was intended as a technique for sharpening young minds, but was regarded by many as off-putting and time-wasting. Elijah shared this opinion. Although he emphasized the importance of close and critical study of the Talmud, he understood the text in the light of genuine parallels and he used the work of earlier authorities to illumine difficult passages. He applied methods of biblical interpretation to the Mishnah and he regarded the Palestinian Talmud as being of equal importance to the Babylonian. As a result of his efforts, he was known as the 'Father of Talmud Criticism', and he was a major figure in the revival of strict talmudic learning. Altogether he wrote seventy books, and his annotations of the Talmud are now printed in standard editions alongside the text. In Lithuania particularly, a rich Yiddish culture grew up that rejected the emotionalism of Hasidism in favour of serious scholarship and devotion to the halakhah, and which was characterized by a wry sense of the absurdity of life. Through the influence of Hollywood in the twentieth century, Jewish humour is now appreciated throughout the world and is one highly influential legacy of the Mitnaggdim.

5. THE SHTETL, THE YESHIVAH AND THE MUSAR MOVEMENT

A shtetl was a small town predominantly inhabited by Jews. Its population could vary in size between 1,000 and 20,000, and it provided a regular pattern of living for the Ashkenazi Jews of Eastern Europe from the seventeenth to the late nineteenth century. In Poland, these Jewish towns had developed under the protection of the nobles, but shtetlakh also existed in Lithuania, in the Russian Pale of Settlement and in Austria-Hungary. The towns had their own characteristic values, the most important of which were 'Yiddishkeit' (Jewishness) and 'menschlikheit' (humanness). The synagogue was the central institution, and there the Jew prayed regularly to his God and studied the Torah. Women and men prayed separately, and among the men there was a clear hierarchy of seating with those who were rich, learned and respected placed near the Ark while the beggars and the indigent stayed near the far door.

At home, Jewish rituals were practised and family life emphasized. To a large extent, marriages were arranged by the parents and the local shadchan (matchmaker). There was little privacy, and the whole community was closely involved with the affairs of each individual family. Inevitably, the Jews also came into contact with their non-Jewish neighbours in the market-place, but the goyim (gentiles) were regarded with suspicion. Any interaction might all too easily end in a riot, a pogrom or a massacre.

The institutions of shtetl life were slowly eroded in the early twentieth century and were finally destroyed in the Holocaust. Nevertheless, the values of the shtetl persisted among Jews who emigrated to Israel and the United States. Even today there is nostalgia for the close-knit communities of the past, which is reflected in the enduring popularity of the stories of Sholem Aleichem, the paintings of Marc Chagall and such theatrical productions as *Yentl* and *Fiddler on the Roof*.

Talmudic studies were preserved in the yeshivot (academies). If at all possible, Jewish families would send their sons to study in a yeshivah under the supervision of a prominent rabbi. The students either paid their own way or were supported by the community, and it was considered meritorious to entertain poor yeshivah students for dinner. The Hasidic Tsaddikim kept their own yeshivot, which taught the particular doctrines of the Tsaddik, and the Mitnaggdim also supported yeshivot. Initially pilpul was the main method of teaching (see Part 4), but later yeshivot followed the method of study of the Vilna Gaon and several new institutions were opened in the early nineteenth century. The graduates were not only prepared for the rabbinate; many turned to secular occupations after a few years at a yeshivah, and the intellectual discipline of talmudic study was seen as an excellent preparation for many future careers. At the very least, a yeshivah education was intended to encourage a lifelong devotion to study and provide a glimpse into the joys of meditating on and becoming immersed in the laws of God.

In the nineteenth century, particularly in Lithuania, the study of ethics was added to the yeshivah curriculum. In Mitnaggdim circles, the quality of religious life was being increasingly eroded, partly by the harsh economic conditions of shtetl life in Eastern Europe and partly by the impact of the secular Enlightenment (see Chapter 10, Part 2). Under the leadership of Israel Lipkin (1810–1883), many yeshivot supplemented traditional talmudic teaching with the study of Jewish ethical texts. Lipkin, who for many years had lived in Vilna, was concerned that there was too much concentration on the ritual precepts of Judaism, and in order to redress the balance, he stressed that there was no distinction between the ritual and the ethical and that learning was not intended merely to develop the intellect – it was also meant to encourage certain traits of character and improve standards of behaviour in the community. His students spent half an hour every day reading books of musar (ethics); a mashgi'ah (supervisor) was appointed to look after the moral development of the boys, and the pupils were taught to keep ethical diaries recording their own personal struggles. Lipkin's ideas were taken up in yeshivot all over Lithuania, and today musar is regarded as an essential study in all non-Hasidic academies.

SUGGESTED FURTHER READING

D. Ben-Amos and J.R. Mintz, eds., *In Praise of the Baal Shem Tov*, Indiana University Press, 1970.

L.S. Dawidowicz, *The Golden Tradition: Jewish Life and Thought in Eastern Europe*, Holt, Rinehart and Winston, 1966.

S. Dubnow, *History of the Jews in Russia and Poland*, Ktav, 1973.

H.M. Rabinowicz, *Guide to Hasidism*, Vallentine Mitchell, 1960.

10 THE ENLIGHTENMENT AND PROGRESSIVE JUDAISM

1. THE JEWISH COMMUNITY IN WESTERN EUROPE

While the Hasidim and the Mitnaggdim fought for the soul of eastern European Jewry, momentous changes were occurring in the West. Until the eighteenth century the Jews of western Europe lived very much as they had done in the Middle Ages; they dwelt in societies where monarchs continued to rule by divine right, the aristocracy enjoyed special privileges and were largely exempt from taxation, the Church controlled most educational institutions and the mercantile and craft guilds were closed to outsiders. The Christian peasantry remained in a state of feudal servitude and, in most countries, Jews were confined to special areas of residence and were compelled to wear distinctive clothing. England and Holland were exceptional in that the government did not interfere with the religious life of the Jewish population, but even in England Jews could hold no public office and were not admitted to the universities.

By the 1770s and 1780s, however, the lot of Jews in central Europe began to improve. The Christian writer Wilhelm Christian Dohm (1751–1820) produced an important pamphlet entitled *Concerning the Amelioration of the Civil Status of the Jews*. In it he argued that Jews could become valuable citizens if all occupations and educational institutions were open to them. The Holy Roman Emperor Joseph II (1741–1790) agreed with these sentiments. In 1781, the Jewish badge was abolished and an edict of toleration was issued; the Jews of Vienna were granted freedom in trade and industry, were given permission to live outside the traditional Jewish quarter and were allowed to send their children to state schools. In 1784 Jewish judicial autonomy was abolished, and three years later Jews were inducted into the imperial army for the first time.

Similar reforms took place in France. In 1789 the National Assembly issued a declaration proclaiming that all men are born and remain free. It laid down that, provided they do not subvert civil law, no religious opinions should be persecuted. Two years later, the Assembly granted full citizenship rights to all Jews, and pronounced that all 'adjournments, restrictions and exceptions contained in the preceding decrees affecting individuals of the Jewish persuasion' should be abolished. In 1799, Napoleon became the First Consul of France and was then proclaimed Emperor in 1804; his Code of Civil Law established the right of all citizens to follow any trade. In 1806 he took the extraordinary step of convening an Assembly of Jewish Notables. Traditionally, in Christian Europe the Jews had regulated and administered their own laws. The question now arose whether it was possible for Jews to be full citizens; discussion centred round such issues as the status of Jewish marriage and divorce and the nature of Jewish patriotism. The Jews invoked the ancient halakhic principle 'Dina Malkhuta Dina' (the law of the land is the law). Jewish law, they insisted, was compatible with civil law and the French Jewish community was composed of loyal Frenchmen. The following year Napoleon revived the Sanhedrin (see Chapter 4, Part 4), which was composed both of rabbis and prominent laymen, and it pledged its allegiance to the Emperor and nullified any features of the Jewish tradition that conflicted with the requirements of citizenship. Subsequently, the French Jewish community was organized much as if it were a department of the Civil Service.

After Napoleon's defeat at the Battle of Waterloo, the Great Powers tried to recreate the map of Europe as it had been in the eighteenth century, but nonetheless a resolution was passed at the Congress of Vienna instructing the German states to improve the condition of the Jews. Many German intellectuals regarded Jews as 'Asiatic aliens', however, and maintained that it was impossible to be part of mainstream German culture without being Christian; in 1819 there were serious anti-Jewish riots in several German cities.

After 1830 more liberal views began to prevail. The rights of Jews were argued by people such as Gabriel Riesser (1806–1863) and Heinrich Heine (1797–1856) – Heine was himself a Jewish convert to

Christianity. In 1848 there were revolutions all over Europe, and in Prussia, Austria, Italy, Hungary and Bohemia absolutist rulers were compelled to grant freedoms of speech, assembly and religion to their subjects. Although many of these uprisings had been suppressed, in 1869 the Parliament of the North German Federation proclaimed Jewish emancipation and by 1871 all restrictions concerning occupation, marriage, residence and franchise were removed. Jews became full citizens of the German Reich.

2. THE HASKALAH

Haskalah is the term used for the Jewish Enlightenment, which took place in western Europe in the late eighteenth and early nineteenth centuries. The roots of the Haskalah, however, go back to seventeenth-century Holland, where a number of Jewish intellectuals attempted to understand their religious tradition in the light of current scientific progress.

Dutch Jewry was particularly secure and successful at this time – the beautiful synagogues still standing in Amsterdam today give some idea of the size and wealth of the community. It was a centre for Hebrew publishing, and there was a famous Talmud Torah school with a congregation including physicians, playwrights, financiers and merchants. The community had been enriched by Marrano refugees expelled from the Iberian peninsula (see Chapter 6, Part 5) and by Poles fleeing the Chmielnicki massacres (see Chapter 9, Part 1). There was both a large Sephardic synagogue and several Ashkenazi congregations.

Most famous of these Dutch Jewish thinkers was Baruch Spinoza (1632–1677) who was descended from a Portuguese Marrano family. In his *Theological Political Treatise* he suggested that the Torah was not composed in its entirety by Moses, causing such a storm in the community that his *Ethics* was not published until after his death. Although his works were proscribed by the Jewish establishment, they provide a background to the philosophical ideas of Moses Mendelssohn (1729–1786), who was to prove the most influential thinker of the Haskalah.

Mendelssohn himself was encouraged by the Christian philosopher G. E. Lessing, who became a close personal friend and facilitated the publication of his work. He was convinced that the existence of God, divine providence and the immortality of the soul could all be discovered by the exercise of natural reason. In his *Jerusalem*, he argued for the separation of the state from religion and for freedom of worship, and he maintained that the Jewish people had a unique mission, namely 'to call wholesome and unadulterated ideas of God and His attributes continuously to the attention of the rest of mankind'. Despite his gentile contacts, Mendelssohn was a respected member of the Berlin Jewish community and he always insisted that 'I cannot understand how those who were born into the household of Jacob can in good conscience exempt themselves from the observance of the law'. Thus he himself succeeded in combining traditional observance with being part of the mainstream of western culture.

Mendelssohn realized that if Jews were to become full citizens, they must be comfortable in the modern world. To this end he translated the Pentateuch into German and completed a biblical commentary giving a rational explanation of the Torah. He also encouraged the modernization of Jewish education and, as a result of his efforts, a Jewish free school opened in Berlin in 1781, teaching secular as well as religious subjects. Following his example, a number of Jewish intellectuals known as the Maskilim set up further schools and began publishing the first Jewish literary magazine in order to disseminate their views. There is no doubt that Mendelssohn himself was widely admired, and he was almost certainly the model for Lessing's *Nathan the Wise*. Through his leadership, German Jewry was introduced to secular European culture. But his own family life illustrates the fundamental conflict of emancipation; faced with the temptations of complete assimilation, four out of his six children embraced Christianity later in their lives.

By the 1820s the centre of the Haskalah movement had shifted to Vienna, where the journals *First Fruits of the Times* (1821–1832) and the *Vineyard of Delight* (1833–1856) were published. The fundamental ideas of the contributors were that secular studies should be an essential part of the education of a Jewish child; that Jews should be thoroughly familiar with the language of their adopted countries; that Hebrew rather than Yiddish is the language of the Jews; and that the Jewish religion must adapt itself to the conditions of the modern world.

Increasingly, the Maskilim also argued for the creation of a Jewish homeland. Moses Mendelssohn had prophetically believed that such an aspiration was unrealistic unless or until there was a major European war, but the hope continued to be nurtured. This must be seen in part as a rejection of traditional religious messianic movements such as that of

Shabbetai Zevi (see Chapter 8, Part 5), but it was also the beginning of a modern secular nationalism that would find its fulfilment in Zionism and the creation of the State of Israel.

3. THE GROWTH OF THE REFORM MOVEMENT

Moses Mendelssohn remained an Orthodox Jew, but he created a climate in which non-Orthodox opinion could flourish. The Haskalah had brought major changes to the lives of the Jews of western Europe; they were no longer insulated from mainstream secular civilization and many increasingly felt that traditional forms of worship were irrelevant and unbecoming.

At the beginning of the nineteenth century, the financier Israel Jacobson (1768–1828) initiated a programme of reform. He founded a series of schools throughout the kingdom of Westphalia in which secular studies were taught by gentiles and Jewish studies by Jews. In addition, he built the first Reform temple in Seesen, and services there included choral singing and hymns and prayers in German rather than in the traditional Hebrew. This was closed down during the Emperor Napoleon's occupation of the area, but he later transferred it to Berlin, and meanwhile another Reform temple was established in Hamburg in 1818 with the congregation issuing its own Prayer Book. Repetitious prayers were omitted, and much of the old liturgy that looked for the restoration of Zion and the coming of the Messiah was cut out altogether – if Jews were to be good Germans, there could be no question of a dual loyalty. The reformers had secured several rabbinical opinions justifying their activities, but nonetheless the representatives of the old traditional ways were appalled. The authority of the Prussian government was invoked, the temple in Berlin was forbidden to hold services and in 1823 a decree was issued forbidding any innovation in services.

With increasing flexibility in the structure of autonomous Jewish life, however, the Orthodox could not enforce their prohibition everywhere. The Bet Din (rabbinic court) of Prague, for example, made harsh declarations about the people of the Hamburg temple: 'It is their entire desire to parade before the Christians as being more learned than their brothers. Basically they have no religion at all.' Yet there was nothing concrete they could do, and the Hamburg temple continued to attract members. Services were performed with far more ceremony and decorum than was usual in synagogues; there was a choir; the liturgy was shorter and the congregation prayed in unison.

Many German rabbis were influenced by the new trends. Scholars such as Leopold Zunz (1794–1886) were involved in the scientific study of Judaism (Wissenchaft des Judentums), an attempt to study the Jewish tradition with no religious preconceptions. It was no longer to be taken as an immutable truth that the whole written and oral law was handed down complete and perfect by God to Moses on Mount Sinai; the idea that Judaism, like everything else, was subject to the historical process was extremely influential among those Jews who had, for the first time, experienced a full secular education.

In 1838, amid great controversy, Abraham Geiger (1810–1874) – who had organized the first conference for Reform rabbis – was appointed second rabbi of Breslau. He formulated the principles on which the new movement should rest, arguing that the essence of Judaism was ethical monotheism and that many traditional doctrines and practices no longer had any meaning or validity. In fact Geiger was more orthodox in his actions than in his opinions, but this was not true of his contemporary Samuel Holdheim (1806–1866) who founded the Association for Reform Judaism. He was in favour of transferring the Jewish Sabbath from Saturday to Sunday, of praying with the head uncovered and of the modification of the dietary laws. Reform Judaism spread beyond Germany, and in England the West London Synagogue for Reform Jews was founded in 1841.

In 1854 a Reform rabbinical seminary was founded for the new movement at Breslau, based on free historical enquiry coupled with a real commitment to the Jewish tradition. Its first principal was Zacharias Frankel of Dresden (1801–1875), who was considered to be more conservative than many Reform rabbis. Further rabbinical conferences took place and such subjects as the dietary laws, the Sabbath, the status of mixed marriages and the role of Hebrew in the liturgy were discussed. In 1867 another moderate Reform rabbinical seminary was opened in Hungary, where a particular form of Reform Judaism known as Neologism was practised. In 1872, the Berlin Hochschule was created under the direction of Abraham Geiger, and the Union of Liberal Rabbis of Germany was formed in 1899. Thus, despite the disapproval of the traditionalists, non-Orthodox Judaism was firmly established in western Europe by the end of the nineteenth century.

4. THE DEVELOPMENT OF REFORM JUDAISM IN THE UNITED STATES

The early Jewish settlers of the United States were mainly Sephardim, coming from Spain, North Africa, Holland and Turkey. In the early nineteenth century, however, German Jews began to emigrate and many of them had been influenced by the Reform movement in western Europe. The first signs of change appeared in 1824 in Charleston, South Carolina, where a small group tried to introduce new liturgical practices similar to those of the Hamburg temple. As one of these early reformers said, their intention was 'to take away everything that might excite the disgust of the well-informed Israelites'.

The revolutionary fervour of the 1840s in Europe led to more emigration, with New York frequently the first stopping place. By 1842 there were three German synagogues in the city, and in 1845 Temple Emmanuel was founded, immediately introducing new forms of worship in the Reform pattern. The process was repeated in several cities and was encouraged by a group of Reform rabbis who had taken part in the Reform rabbinical conferences and had subsequently settled in the United States. Prominent among these were Samuel Hirsch (1815–1889), who had been Chief Rabbi of Luxembourg before taking the pulpit of Temple Kenesset Israel in Philadelphia; David Einhorn (1809–1879) of Har Sinai, Baltimore; and Samuel Adler (1809–1891) and Gustav Gottheil (1827–1903), co-rabbis of Temple Emmanuel, New York. Perhaps the most influential was Isaac Mayer Wise (1819–1900), who came to America to serve Temple Beth El of Albany, New York, later moving to Cincinnati, Ohio, where he founded the English-language weekly, *The Israelite*, as well as a German periodical. He also produced a new Prayer Book, *Minhag America* ('American Custom') and as early as 1855 he made a first attempt to found a rabbinical college. This proved to be a failure, but he then directed his energy towards forming a rabbinical union, and the first conference of American rabbis took place in Philadelphia in 1869, followed by the creation of a permanent organization known as the Union of American Hebrew Congregations (UAHC). In 1875 Wise succeeded in founding in Cincinnati the first American rabbinical seminary, the Hebrew Union College.

The time had come for a formal declaration of the principles of American Reform Judaism. In Europe, men such as Abraham Geiger (see

Part 3), Heinrich Graetz (1817–1891) in his *History of the Jews*, and Samuel Hirsch in *Religious Philosophy of the Jews*, had attempted to devise a progressive understanding of Jewish history. At the European conferences the practical implications of the new ideas were discussed. In Pittsburgh in 1885 a new Reform platform was produced, and under the chairmanship of Kaufman Kohler (1843–1926), fifteen rabbis deliberated on the principles of the movement. It was agreed that the Jewish religion needed to be modernized to take into account the findings of modern scientists, anthropologists, historians and biblical critics; although the moral laws of the Bible were binding for all time, only rituals found to be spiritually uplifting needed to be retained, they decided. The dietary laws, the laws of ritual purity and the laws of dress were rejected as anachronistic. The expectation of a future personal Messiah was eliminated, as were the doctrines of the resurrection of the body and everlasting reward and punishment. Instead, Reform Jews were to look for the establishment of justice and peace for all humanity here on earth, and were to build a progressive religion, 'ever striving to be in accord with the postulates of reason'. Finally, there was a firm commitment to the duty of social action, which was to become a major focus for later Reform congregational activity.

The Pittsburgh Platform, as it came to be called, together with the Hebrew Union College and the Union of American Hebrew Congregations, provided a framework for the growth and development of Reform Judaism for the next fifty years. By the latter half of the nineteenth century, Jewish existence in both the United States and western Europe had been transformed by the forces of emancipation, with many Jews becoming indistinguishable from their fellow citizens. They no longer ate special food, wore distinctive clothes or practised unusual customs, they had full civil rights, and they were ready to make their contribution to secular society.

5. OPPOSITION TO REFORM

The reformers did not carry all before them. The term 'Orthodox' is a comparatively modern one in the history of Judaism; before the eighteenth century, with the exception of a few heretics such as the Karaites (see Chapter 6, Part 3), all Jews believed that the entire written and oral law was given to Moses on Mount Sinai, and that the Jews were a special people, God's chosen ones who had literally been sanctified by His commandments. By the nineteenth century this unwavering conviction had been called into doubt, and the term 'Orthodox' came to be used to distinguish those who remained faithful to the old tradition from the adherents of the new Reform movement. The Orthodox thus perceived themselves as the true guardians of Torah.

From the beginning of the Haskalah, many Orthodox leaders feared the breaking down of the ghetto walls, because they realized that participation in mainstream secular culture would lead to innumerable temptations. At one stage the faithful were banned even from reading Moses Mendelssohn's German translation of the Pentateuch. Mendelssohn was known to be a pious scholar and an observant Jew, but dabbling in German culture was thought to lead inevitably to assimilation, or worse. These fears were somewhat justified by the numerous conversions to Christianity that occurred at this time; not only four of Mendelssohn's children, but the poet Heinrich Heine and the legal historian Eduard Gans were prominent examples of those who succumbed.

Most influential among the German Orthodox thinkers was Samson Raphael Hirsch (1808–1888). He had had an excellent secular education at a German school and at the University of Bonn. At the age of twenty-two he had been appointed Chief Rabbi of the Duchy of Odenburg, and in 1836 he published a defence of traditional Judaism entitled *The Nineteen Letters on Judaism,* in which he argued that the purpose of human life is not to attain personal happiness, but rather to obey the will of God. The mission of the Jewish people, he wrote, is to illustrate to the rest of humanity that joy is to be found in obedience, and that following the commandments does not exclude the possibility of material prosperity, for Judaism is not an ascetic religion. Hirsch believed that political emancipation was of little importance, for ultimately, he insisted, God 'would unite again His servants in one land, and the Torah shall be the guiding principle of a state, a model of the meaning of divine revelation and the mission of humanity'. Clearly, if the role of the Jewish people was to provide a model of brotherhood under the law for the world, then the Reform movement could only be condemned.

Immediately this raised a serious problem. According to Jewish law, one is Jewish if one's mother is Jewish, and with the exception of converts, the criterion of Jewishness has never been anything but one of biological descent. In that sense, obedience or disobedience is irrelevant. By the halakhic criteria, the Reform movement was doing nothing to splinter the community; both Orthodox and Reform were descended from Abraham, recognized themselves as Jews and arguably could work together on community projects. On the other hand, working with and indeed even associating with adherents of Reform implied that there could be different forms of Judaism. Susceptible young people might be led astray – the Jews would no longer be the People of the Book.

Hirsch himself decided upon a separatist path, and in 1876 the Orthodox in Germany set up separate organizations for their members. It was acknowledged that the ideal of K'lal Israel (the complete community of Israel) was broken, but at the same time Hirsch did not divorce himself completely from the secular world – he did believe that it was possible to be a fully observant Jew and also to be conversant with modern culture. This position came to be known as neo-Orthodoxy. There could be no compromise on the doctrine of Torah mi-Sinai (God's law from Sinai), and all Reform practices must be unequivocally rejected, but at the same time, Jews could have the benefit of a secular education.

Although both the Reform and the neo-Orthodox were highly influential in western Europe and the United States, it must be remembered that until World War I there was little change in the shtetlakh and yeshivot of Poland and Russia. There, the old ways of life continued – change was on the horizon, but it was not to be prompted by political emancipation. Rather, it occurred in response to both anti-Semitism and to the chance of a new life across the Atlantic Ocean.

SUGGESTED FURTHER READING

J. Katz, *Out of the Ghetto: The Social Background of Jewish Emancipation*, Harvard University Press, 1973.
D. Phillipson, *The Reform Movement in Judaism*, Ktav, 1967.
G.W. Plaut, ed., *The Rise of Reform Judaism*, WUPJ, 1963.
G.W. Plaut, ed., *The Growth of Reform Judaism*, WUPJ, 1965.
H.M. Sachar, *The Course of Modern Jewish History*, Delta, 1958.

11 ANTI-SEMITISM AND ZIONISM

1. THE RISE OF ANTI-SEMITISM

By the second half of the nineteenth century, Jewish life in western Europe had been transformed. Jews were no longer a visibly distinctive minority group; they had full civil rights, mingled freely with their gentile neighbours and played their part in the political, economic and cultural life of their host nations. Most reformers believed that this situation would ultimately end anti-Jewish sentiment, but sadly this was not to be the case. In the final decades of the century, even greater hostility towards the Jewish community emerged for a variety of reasons.

The term 'anti-Semitism' was first coined by the German journalist Wilhelm Marr in the 1870s. Previously, hatred of Jews had been accorded a religious justification; they had rejected the salvation offered in Jesus and they were popularly condemned as Christ-killers. Marr's conception was rather different. He insisted that the Jews were a biologically alien people, unassimilable because they were of a different and foreign race; he held that modern history should be understood as an ongoing struggle between the 'Semitic alien' and 'native Teutonic stock'.

In the 1870s, conditions all over Europe were unsettled. Several newly independent nations emerged, each determined to maintain its distinctive national identity, and indigenous minority groups of all kinds were all too often subject to persecution because they were seen as a threat to the ruling majority. Jews in particular were regarded as oriental intruders.

In Germany, many Jews had done well in the more liberal political climate. In 1878 a Christian social party was founded, claiming that the press and the financial institutions were controlled by Jews, who were therefore responsible for all the nation's current economic difficulties. This argument proved very attractive to many shopkeepers, artisans and clerks, and by 1881 it was being claimed publicly that the Jewish physical type constituted a biological threat to the pure-bred German nation. Petitions were organized to prevent any further immigration. By the 1890s, sixteen deputies had been elected to the German Reichstag on anti-Semitic tickets.

Anti-Semitism was also fashionable in France. Anti-Jewish feeling had previously been exploited from time to time by monarchists and traditional Catholic clergy to combat the liberal ideas that had first emerged at the time of the Revolution, but it was the Dreyfus case that brought the issue into the national forum. In 1894, Alfred Dreyfus – a high-ranking Jewish army officer – was found guilty of high treason and sentenced to life imprisonment. He consistently protested his innocence and subsequently it was discovered that the documents upon which his conviction was based had been forged. France was divided on the issue. Many remained convinced of his guilt, and saw him as part of a Jewish conspiracy to undermine the stability of France, while others insisted that the whole affair was a gross miscarriage of justice. The matter dragged on, and when Dreyfus was tried again in 1899 a second guilty verdict was returned, although extenuating circumstances were admitted. He was given a personal pardon by the French president, but it was not until 1906 that the Court of Cassation finally vindicated him. For many Jews, including Theodor Herzl (see Part 3), the whole affair demonstrated the latent anti-Semitism simmering in 'emancipated' Europe.

In Russia, anti-Semitism became official state policy. After Czar Alexander II was assassinated in 1881, the Ministry of the Interior decreed a series of laws that curtailed Jewish rights of residence in the Pale of Settlement. By the late 1880s, strict quotas were being imposed on Jewish admission to the universities and professions, and in 1891 more than 20,000 Jews were expelled from Moscow. Meanwhile a number of writers were expounding explicitly anti-Semitic racial theories; the Jew was described as innately egoistic, mercenary, materialistic, cowardly and culturally degenerate. The most influential of these works was the anonymous *Protocols of the Elders of Zion*, circulated in Russian official circles from the late 1880s, and purporting to be the documents of a clandestine Jewish organization bent on world domination through the financial institutions and the press. Although proved to be a forgery, the Protocols remains in circulation in many countries even today. Currently, it is enjoying a revival in the newly independent states of the old Soviet Union, and it is also frequently reprinted and widely distributed throughout the Arab world.

2. POGROMS AND EMIGRATION

The word 'pogrom' comes from the Russian language and indicates an attack on one sector of society by another, accompanied by rape, murder and the wilful destruction of property. Although pogroms were carried out against other groups such as the Armenians, the term is specifically used to describe the attacks on the Jews of Eastern Europe between 1881 and 1921. In Russia, in particular, this was a time of political confusion and turmoil, and the outbreaks of violence were linked to nationalist incitement and social upheaval. In general, the civil authorities remained neutral and did little to protect their Jewish countrymen; consequently, much of the Jewish community of Eastern Europe looked to a new life in the United States as the only long-term solution to their problems.

There were three main waves of pogroms in Russia: the first took place between 1881 and 1884. After the assassination of Czar Alexander II, the rumour was circulated that the Jews were responsible, and attacks began in the Ukraine. In Kiev rioting against the Jewish community lasted for three days, with the police doing nothing to control the perpetrators. Unrest spread to Belorussia and Lithuania, and there was also a serious pogrom in Warsaw on Christmas Day, 1881. Although ultimately the administration reacted against the insurgents, the government passed a series of acts severely curtailing Jewish freedoms. There is no doubt that this series of pogroms was a turning-point in the history of Russian Jewry. Mass emigration to the New World began, and many Jews also became caught up in revolutionary and Zionist movements (see Part 4).

The second wave of pogroms took place between 1903 and 1906. This was a time of revolutionary agitation, and increasingly the government allowed the pro-Czarist press to express virulent anti-Semitic sentiments in order to divert the populace from pursuing the need for reform. At Kishinev, forty-five Jews were murdered and about 1,500 Jewish houses and businesses were looted. Unrest spread throughout the Pale of Settlement. At Odessa, more than 300 were killed and further small-scale pogroms took place in more than sixty towns.

The most severe outbreaks, however, took place between 1917 and

1921, during the Revolution and subsequent civil war. The chief perpetrators were the Ukrainian units of the Red Army and the counter-revolutionaries of the White Army, and pogroms occurred in every region from the Ukraine to Siberia. It is impossible to know how many Jews died during this period – possibly as many as 150,000 were killed and many more wounded – but certainly world Jewry was appalled. Within Russia itself, the pogroms converted many Jews to the Red cause, and everywhere they strengthened the desire for an independent Jewish homeland.

By 1880 the Jewish population of the United States stood at approximately 250,000. Between 1881 and 1914, approximately two million Eastern European Jews emigrated to the United States. In addition, 350,000 settled in continental Europe, 200,000 went to the United Kingdom, 40,000 travelled to South Africa, 115,000 to Argentina and 100,000 to Canada. This influx completely changed the composition of the Jewish community in all these countries. In the United States in particular, the newcomers crowded into the big cities, where they had to work in unhealthy conditions. They brought with them all their Yiddish institutions including their strict orthodoxy, and the prosperous, assimilated German Jews found them disconcerting – they were too foreign, too unworldly, too pious, too Jewish. Nonetheless, they felt a sense of responsibility for their co-religionists, and they revived the Jewish Theological Seminary in New York to train modern, yet traditional rabbis. This later became the central institution for Conservative Judaism. They founded the American Jewish Committee to lobby the government on Jewish issues abroad, the Anti-Defamation League to combat anti-Semitism at home, and a host of Jewish charities. Within a couple of generations, the distinction between the old German and the new Russian immigrants had all but disappeared – in a very real sense they had all become Americans.

3. THEODOR HERZL AND THE ZIONIST DREAM

Besides the United States, South America, Canada, South Africa, continental Europe and Britain, many Russian Jews were drawn to the idea of a homeland in Palestine. The old dream of returning to the Promised Land had been retained in the Jewish community. It was expressed in the liturgy – perhaps most poignantly at the Passover meal when the service ends with the words, 'Next year in Jerusalem!'

Traditionally it was connected with the belief in the coming of the Messiah, who would gather the scattered tribes of Israel from the ends of the earth so that ultimately all nations would turn to Jerusalem and recognize the one true God. After the first Russian pogrom in 1882, several thousand Jews left for Palestine, where they worked as shopkeepers and artisans. Other immigrants of the period were employed as farmers and labourers. They were known as Bilu – an acronym from the Hebrew 'House of Jacob, let us go' – and they frequently combined Jewish nationalism with Marxist convictions. In addition, Hibbat Zion ('Love of Zion') societies were organized throughout Russia, Poland and Romania to purchase further land in Palestine for settlement.

At this time, a well-known Russian physician, Leon Pinsker (1821–1891), published a tract entitled *Autoemancipation*, in which he argued that Jewish liberation could only be guaranteed by the establishment of a Jewish political state. Peace between nations, he argued, was dependent on at least token equality between them. Because the Jews were without their own country, they were at a perpetual disadvantage; anti-Semitism was a permanent threat and the Jews' problems would not be solved merely by emigrating to another country, where they would continue to be in a minority. The pamphlet was highly influential, but the real founder of political Zionism was Theodor Herzl (1860–1904).

Herzl was born in Budapest and studied in Vienna. He earned his living as a journalist and became increasingly interested in the Jewish situation. Initially he had believed that complete assimilation into the majority culture would solve the problems, but the Dreyfus trial caused him to revise his opinion. In 1896 he published his *Der Judenstaat* ('The Jewish State') in which he advocated the founding of a Jewish state by international agreement. Palestine was the obvious location for the new nation. Herzl was opposed both by the assimilationists, who believed in being good citizens of the host country, and by the strictly Orthodox who condemned him for anticipating God's plan. Nonetheless many young Jews were inspired by the book, and the Hibbat Zion movement rallied behind him.

In 1897 Herzl convened the First Zionist Congress in Basle and the World Zionist Organization was founded. Herzl himself acted as president, and devoted his energy to building up international support. He met Kaiser Wilhelm II in 1898 and Sultan Abdul Hamid in 1901, but nothing definite was achieved. Herzl was prepared to consider sites other than Palestine; at various times a tract of Turkey, Cyprus, the Sinai Peninsula and areas of Uganda were suggested. This last was given approval by the British and, after a visit to the Pale of Settlement in 1903 where he encountered poverty and deprivation, Herzl reluctantly agreed. But the proposal aroused a storm of protest at the Sixth Zionist Conference, and in 1904, the year of his death, Herzl was compelled to affirm his commitment to Palestine at a plenary session of the Zionist Action Committee. It is probable that the strain of these negotiations finally undermined his health.

The new president of the World Zionist Organization was David Wolffson (1856–1914), who attempted to heal rifts between the competing factions of the movement. Under his leadership, many Orthodox Jews became involved as members of the Mizrachi party. This had been founded in 1901, and was dedicated to the preservation of strictly Orthodox ways within a Jewish state. Socialist Jews also became members through the Poale Zion (the Labour Zionist Party) which was determined to promote a socialist programme. In the 1907 congress, under Wolffson's presidency, a resolution was passed pledging the organization to a quest for a charter, to the achievement of physical settlement in Palestine, and to the revival of the Hebrew language. Opposition to Wolffson's leadership grew, however, from the Russians, who wanted greater emphasis on practical work in Palestine rather than political negotiation, and he was not re-elected to the presidency in 1911.

4. THE ZIONIST MOVEMENT

By the beginning of the twentieth century, a sizeable number of Jews had settled in Palestine. The majority lived in the cities, but some worked in agricultural colonies under the control of the Palestine Jewish Colonization Association. In 1904 a second wave of immigrants departed for the Promised Land after further Russian pogroms and most of these settlers were determined to earn their living by farming. Prominent among this group was Aaron David Gordon (1856–1922) who declared 'too long have the hands been the hands of Esau and the voice the voice of Jacob. It is time for Jacob to use his hands too.' There was a determination from the earliest days to create a Hebrew rather than a Yiddish culture. Children were educated in Hebrew-language schools and used Hebrew as their daily language; the philologist Ben Yehuda (1858–1922) produced a dictionary of modern Hebrew; and a new Hebrew literature began to be created through the work of such writers as Asher Ginsberg, known as Ahad Ha-Am (1856–1927), Reuben Brainin (1862–1939) and Chaim Nachman Bialik (1873–1934). By the end of World War I, the Jewish community in Palestine numbered approximately 90,000.

From the earliest days of Zionism, there were various different parties within the movement. The political wing and the World Zionist Organization were essentially secular in both their inspiration and aspirations; Herzl himself believed that a Jewish state was a political necessity if Jews were to escape from recurrent bursts of anti-Semitism. Admittedly some early writers such as Judah Alkali (1798–1878) in his booklet *Shema Yisrael* ('Hear O Israel') and Tzevi Hirsch Kalischer (1795–1874) in his *Derishat Zion* ('Seeking Zion') attempted to justify a human-inspired return to Zion on religious grounds, but they were in the minority. In general Herzl's movement ignored the religious aspects of Judaism and emphasized the political needs of the people of Israel. At the Fifth Zionist Conference in 1901, some western European delegates adopted a specifically anti-religious stance, and in response Rabbi Isaac Reines of Poland formed the Mizrachi party, the religious wing of the Zionist movement. The motto of the Mizrachi was 'The Land of Israel to the People of Israel according to the Law of Israel'. The photographs of early Mizrachi conferences in Poland show splendid groups of strictly Orthodox gentlemen, all imposingly clad in dark suits and black hats, all bearded, and without a woman in sight. The co-operation between the secular Zionists and the Mizrachi aroused opposition from many leading rabbis of the time, particularly among the Hasidim.

In 1911 the Tenth Zionist Conference passed a motion making itself responsible for educational and cultural activities. Many members of the Mizrachi were appalled, since education was traditionally the preserve of the religious authorities. In 1912 a conference was held at Kattowitz which founded the Agudat Israel, opposing any form of political Zionism. The Agudat was determined not to co-operate with the World Zionist Organization. It formed branches in all leading European communities to support institutions of Orthodox Jewish learning, and over the years men's, women's and children's divisions have been founded. Subsequently socialist groups emerged from both the Mizrachi and the Agudat Israel, known as the Poel Mizrachi and the Poalei Agudat Israel respectively. Since the foundation of the State of Israel, all four religious parties have fielded candidates in the elections.

Meanwhile, other Zionists emphasized not political or religious, but cultural nationalism. Foremost among these was Ahad Ha-Am, who maintained that the love of Zion 'stands for a Judaism which shall have as its focal point the ideal of our nation's unity, its renaissance and its free development through the expression of universal human values in terms of its own distinctive spirit'. He believed Jewish existence was grounded not in the Jewish religion, but in Jewish civilization. This, however, was rejected by socialists such as Nahman Syrkin (1868–1924), who insisted that the role of Zionism was to create a socialist state in Palestine with values based on the biblical concept of justice. The socialist homeland would be a secularized version of the messianic vision. Another influential socialist thinker was Ber Borochov (1881–1917), who was a founder and leader of the Poale Zion party. This was actively engaged in the Diaspora with the democratization of Jewish communal life, and in Palestine it worked for collective settlements such as the kevutzot (the forerunners of the kibbutzim) and encouraged the growth of trade unionism.

5. THE IMPACT OF WORLD WAR I ON THE JEWISH COMMUNITY

In World War I – which changed the social order of every country it touched – Jews served in the armies of their host nations on both sides. After the war, European centres of population had been profoundly altered. Approximately three million Jews now lived in reconstituted Poland; 445,000 in Hungary; 850,000 in the expanded Romania; 95,000 in Latvia; 115,000 in Lithuania; 375,000 in Czechoslovakia; 191,000 in Austria; 68,000 in Yugoslavia; 48,000 in Bulgaria; and 73,000 in Greece. In all these countries, property had been destroyed, large markets had been replaced by smaller economic units and protective tariffs were introduced. In every case Jews became more vulnerable, since governments were determined to foster national interests at the expense of minority groups. More than ever, Jews were viewed as outsiders. Strict quotas were applied for admission to university and the professional schools, Jews were excluded from state bureaucracies and several political parties advocated explicitly anti-Semitic policies. Nonetheless,

Jewish life flourished. New schools, youth movements and yeshivot were founded, and in some countries Jews even formed their own political parties.

Meanwhile in Russia, the Czar had been overthrown in 1917 and Kerinski's provisional government abolished all legal discrimination against Jews. Later, during the civil war, the Red Army tried to discourage anti-Semitic feeling, but the White troops had no hesitation in massacring whole Jewish communities. It has been estimated that during this period between 100,000 and 150,000 Jews were killed in Russia. After the Revolution, the Bolshevik government was avowedly anti-religious, and all specifically Jewish committees and places of religious education were abolished, while at the same time Jewishness was recognized as an ethnic classification. At one stage in the 1920s the region of Birobidzhan was set aside for Jewish colonization and anti-Semitism was forbidden. Nonetheless within a few years Jewish cultural programmes were also disbanded and Jews were removed from party and governmental positions; the Jew remained an easy scapegoat for every social, political and economic ill.

After the war, Jewish immigration to the United States increased, but was later curtailed by restrictive laws passed in 1921 and 1924; other western countries followed a similar policy, and this had an important effect on the Jewish community. The cessation of immigration led to a decline in the Jewish working class and the erosion of Yiddish culture. Immigrants had been anxious that their children should be well-educated and should integrate themselves into the majority culture. As these children grew up to become middle-class and prosperous, many of them attained influential positions in the spheres of politics, business, art, music, film, science and literature. Even in the United States, while certain prestigious residential neighbourhoods and exclusive social clubs remained closed to Jews and the universities and legal and medical schools operated quotas against Jewish candidates, many Jews became highly successful members of American society.

The League of Nations had agreed after the war that Britain would administer Palestine, and the Jews themselves organized a National Assembly and an Executive Council. By 1929, the Palestine Jewish community numbered about 160,000, increasing to nearly half a million by the beginning of World War II. About a quarter of this population lived in co-operative communities, and the cities of Tel Aviv, Jerusalem and Haifa were well settled. Industrialization was initiated by the Palestine Electric Corporation and was developed by the Histradrut – the General Federation of Hebrew Workers. The Hebrew University was opened in 1925. Between the wars, approximately one million Arabs were also living in Palestine, and in 1929 they rioted against the Jews. Despite the Balfour Declaration of 1917, in which the British Government had declared its support for 'the establishment in Palestine of a national home for the Jewish people' and promised to 'use their best endeavours to facilitate the achievement of this object', the British used their powers after the riots to cut down Jewish immigration. By 1936, many Arabs, supported by Syria, Iraq and Egypt, were launching a concerted offensive against the Jewish settlers.

In the late 1920s, the various socialist and labour groups had joined together to form the Israel Labour Party. Chaim Weizman (1874–1952) was president of the World Zionist Organization and tried to co-operate with the British. A significant minority, led by Vladimir Jabotinsky (1880–1940) and known as the Union of Zionist Revisionists, would allow no compromise. They were determined to work single-mindedly for the establishment of an independent Jewish state, and in 1935 they formed an alternative organization, withdrawing their members from the Jewish militia (the Haganah) to form their own group (the Irgun). In 1937 a British Royal Commission advocated that Palestine be partitioned into a Jewish and an Arab state, but this was rejected in a 1939 White Paper that limited Jewish immigration further and promised independence to Palestine within the next ten years. That was where matters stood when World War II was poised to break out over Europe.

SUGGESTED FURTHER READING

D. Cohn-Sherbok, *Israel: The History of an Idea*, SPCK, 1992.
D. Cohn-Sherbok, *The Crucified Jew*, Harper Collins, 1992.
N. Glazer, *American Judaism*, University of Chicago Press, 1972.
W. Laqueur, *A History of Zionism*, Schocken, 1976.

12 THE HOLOCAUST AND ITS AFTERMATH

1. NAZI ANTI-SEMITISM

Between 1930 and 1933, over six million people were unemployed in Germany; it was the time of the Great Depression. During the last days of World War I, Germany had adopted a new constitution and declared itself a federal republic. As a result of the economic crises of the early 1930s, the government increasingly began to rule by presidential decree and in 1933, after several less than effective coalitions, Field-Marshal Paul von Hindenburg appointed Adolf Hitler, the leader of the National Socialist party, Chancellor of Germany.

During the 1920s, the National Socialists had been only a minor force in German politics. The party's ideology was based on a fusion of anti-Jewish sentiment and anti-Communism – Hitler was convinced that all Jews were parasites and degenerates, believed that Germany had lost the war because of the treachery of Jewish socialists, liberals and pacifists, and maintained that the Bolshevik Revolution in Russia was part of a world-wide Jewish plot. He insisted that Germany was entitled to greater living space in the East and that, under Communism, the Jews had achieved power over the Slavs. What was needed, he claimed, was an Aryan victory, to give true-born Germans the power and empire that was their rightful due. This message of intense German patriotism coupled with virulent anti-Semitism had an appeal for industrialists who feared Communism, for the socially insecure, and for the young who were eager for action and glory. In 1929 the Nazis had received less than a million votes, but by 1933 they had gained the support of over forty-four per cent of the electorate and had become the largest single party in the Reichstag.

The revival of anti-Semitism was not confined to Germany. In Russia, the *Protocols of the Elders of Zion* (see Chapter 11, Part 1) was widely circulated and the Jews were generally believed to be responsible for the murder of the Czar; in Britain such popular writers as Kipling, Belloc and G. K. Chesterton expressed openly anti-Semitic sentiments; and in the United States, particularly the 1920s and 30s, anti-Semitic sentiments were frequently expressed even in educated gentile circles. In France too, the idea of a world-wide Jewish conspiracy was much discussed. These anti-Semitic attitudes crystallized in Hitler's own conception of the Jew as a member of a demonic race seeking world domination. He described his feelings thus:

> With satanic joy in his face, the black-haired Jewish youth
> lurks in wait for the unsuspecting girl whom he defiles with his
> blood . . . With every means he tries to destroy the racial
> foundations of the people he has set out to subjugate . . . it was
> and it is Jews who bring the Negroes into the Rhineland, always
> with the same secret and clear aim of ruining the hated white race
> by the necessarily resulting bastardization, throwing it down
> from its cultural and political heights, and himself rising to be its
> master.

Once the Nazi party gained power, it instituted a series of anti-Jewish measures. In May 1933, book burnings took place and several eminent scholars and scientists were arrested. In 1935, all sexual liaisons between Jews and non-Jews were classified as crimes against the state. By 1938, all Jewish communal bodies were put under the direct control of the Nazi secret police, the Gestapo, and all Jews were forced to register their property. Then, later in the same year, the Nazi party organized a concerted attack against the Jewish population, and in one night, Jewish shops and businesses were destroyed, synagogues were burned to the ground, and many Jewish individuals were murdered. In many areas the local population did not hesitate to help the Nazi stormtroopers in their orgy of destruction.

For many German Jews this was the end. They tried to find a means of escaping from Germany with their families, but this was not easy, because to pacify the Arabs, the British had placed considerable restriction on immigration to Palestine. Moreover, the United States was suffering a serious economic depression and was accepting very few new citizens, and all the countries of western Europe were in a similar situation – they had massive unemployment and were not inclined to take in any more people. Desperate families did what they could, sometimes sending their children to friends or contacts overseas; others looked as far afield as South Africa, the West Indies or South America for a safe haven. All too many, however, were forced to stay.

2. THE FINAL SOLUTION

Once the Nazis had invaded Poland in September 1939, the full horror of Hitler's plan for the Jews was revealed. In response to the invasion, the Allied Powers had declared war on Germany, so there was no longer any possibility of escape by emigration to other countries. Poland had a very large Jewish population, and in every conquered town the Jews were seized and forced to clear rubble, carry heavy loads, and scrub floors and lavatories in a massive work programme. They were stripped of their jewellery, and the beards and sideburns traditionally worn by Orthodox Jews were shaved off. The slave-labour operation was described by leading Nazis as 'destruction through work'. The workers toiled for seven days a week; they wore little more than rags, and lived on a meagre diet of bread, soup and potatoes. The death toll was enormous.

At the start of the war, Hitler had signed a non-aggression pact with Stalin, the Russian leader. In 1941, however, Hitler broke this by invading Russia, intending to destroy what he described as the 'Jewish–Bolshevik conspiracy'. Special troops known as the Einsatzgruppen were employed to deal with the Jews. The Einsatzgruppen moved into each newly conquered Russian town, rounded up the Jews in the market-place, marched them out of the town, shot them and buried them in mass graves. Numerous eye-witness accounts of these massacres have been preserved. In the initial sweep between October and December 1941, more than 300,000 Jews were killed in this way; in the second stage lasting through 1942, a further 900,000 were exterminated.

This method of destroying European Jewry, however, was not sufficiently systematic for the Nazis, and from 1941 experiments began to be conducted using poison gas. Initially mobile gas units were sent to each battalion of Einsatzgruppen, but then more permanent arrangements were made. Six death camps were built, at Chelmno, Auschwitz, Sobibor, Majdanek, Treblinka and Belzec. The Nazi leader Goebbels noted: 'A judgment is being visited on the Jews. The prophecy which the

Führer made about them for having brought on a new world war is beginning to come true in the most terrible manner.' People were rounded up, forced into cattle cars with no seating, heating or sanitation and carried by rail on the long journey east. Once they arrived at the camp, the young and fit were selected for work, while the elderly and helpless were gassed immediately.

The figures speak for themselves. The camp at Auschwitz was the central extermination centre for western Europe, and at its greatest capacity it could hold 140,000 inmates, who were systematically worked to death. It also had five crematoria that could dispose of a total of 10,000 bodies per day. Altogether, probably two million people died at Auschwitz.

The whole operation was conducted with ruthless efficiency. Even when Germany was clearly losing the war, nothing was allowed to stand in the way of the transportation of cattle trucks to the east. In general there was little resistance; the Jews were poor, isolated, surrounded by hostile neighbours and terrified. But Warsaw was a notable exception. The Jewish population had been crammed into a small area of the city, and under the leadership of the young Zionist Mordecai Anilewicz, underground shelters were devised and arms were purchased. When the Nazis moved in for the final destruction of the ghetto, they were attacked from all sides. The troops bombarded the buildings, flooded the sewers and released dogs, but for several weeks the Jewish resistance held out against the might of the German Reich. When the inevitable end came, like their co-religionists at Masada (see Chapter 4, Part 5) many chose to commit suicide rather than fall into the hands of the enemy.

By the end of World War II, European Jewry was decimated. It is estimated that ninety per cent of the Jewish population of Poland, Estonia, Latvia, Lithuania, Germany and Austria had been murdered, and more than seventy per cent in occupied Russia, the Ukraine, Belgium, Yugoslavia, Romania and Norway. All too often their gentile neighbours did little to help the Jews – indeed, some were all too anxious to take over their property. The notable exception was Denmark where, in order to save the community, a campaign was launched to transport all the Jews by small boats over the sea to neutral Sweden. But this was a drop in the ocean, and altogether it is estimated that the Nazis killed six million Jews. The old synagogues, yeshivot and places of Jewish learning were destroyed for ever. The life of the shtetl (see Chapter 9, Part 5) was gone from Europe.

3. THE CREATION OF THE STATE OF ISRAEL

The death of six million Jews in the Holocaust and the creation of the State of Israel are two interrelated events. World Jewry was profoundly affected by the catastrophe and, even among Reform Jews, there was a radical shift in opinion towards the Zionist cause. Throughout World War II, the Jewish community had supported the Allies and many American, British and Canadian Jews had served in the Allied army. Nevertheless, Jewry was also committed to overturning British policy in Palestine as expressed in the 1939 White Paper. During the war years the British had tried to prevent illegal Jewish landings in Palestine and would-be emigrants who did get through were often captured later and deported. There were several ugly incidents. In 1942, for example, the *Struma*, a ship carrying Jewish refugees from Romania, was refused permission to land. It was turned back and subsequently sank in the Black Sea with the death of 770 passengers.

In 1943 Menahem Begin (1913–1992) took over the command of the Irgun, the military branch of the Revisionists (see Chapter 11, Part 5). Determined to rid Palestine of the British, he had no hesitation in employing terrorist tactics. On 6 November 1944, an extremist group, the Stern Gang, assassinated Lord Moyne, the British minister for Middle Eastern affairs. Moderate Zionists were aghast, but by 1945, when the full enormity of the Holocaust was realized, a united Jewish Resistance Movement was created. A rift developed between Begin and Chaim Weizman over the bombing of the King David Hotel, where much of the British administration was stationed, but the Irgun continued their campaign, which culminated in the hanging of two British sergeants in retaliation for the hanging of three Jewish terrorists. Exasperated by the whole conflict, the British handed over responsibility to the international community.

In May 1947, the Palestinian question came up for discussion before the United Nations. The then President of the United States, Harry S. Truman, was personally sympathetic to the Jewish cause and was anxious to secure the American Jewish vote in the 1948 presidential election. Eventually, on 29 November, it was agreed that Palestine should be partitioned into a Jewish and an Arab state, and that there should be an international zone in Jerusalem.

Immediately the Arabs began to attack Jewish settlements. Although the Jews were considerably outnumbered and the Palestinian Arabs were aided by extra Egyptian, Syrian, Iraqi and Lebanese troops, the Jews under David Ben Gurion (1886–1973) managed to consolidate their position. They occupied Haifa, opened the route between Tiberius and Eastern Galilee and captured the towns of Safed, Jaffa and Acre. On 14 May 1948, Ben Gurion declared the independence of the Jewish state in Palestine and announced that in future it would be known as the State of Israel. The claim was based on 'national and intrinsic right' as well as on the historic resolution of the United Nations.

For the rest of 1948 the conflict continued despite various truces. The Israelis seized Lydda, Ramleh and Nazareth; they opened the road to the Negev settlements and they took possession of Beersheba. By early 1949 they held large areas beyond the United Nations-designated frontiers. An armistice was eventually signed between Israel on the one side and Egypt, Lebanon, Jordan and Syria on the other, but war broke out again in 1954, in 1967 (when the Israelis captured Jerusalem) and in 1973. There was also the ongoing problem of refugees. In 1947–48, 656,000 Arab inhabitants had fled from Israeli-held territories. Some found sanctuary in the surrounding Arab countries, but others were compelled to live in temporary refugee camps, a constant source of discontent and guerrilla activity.

In 1978, a historic meeting took place between President Sadat of Egypt and Begin, who, as leader of the Likud party, had become Prime Minister of Israel in 1977. Peace was not to be achieved readily. In 1982 Israeli forces invaded Lebanon in order to destroy bases of the Palestine Liberation Organization (PLO) and this destabilized the area. Since 1987, those Palestinians whose homes are in the territories occupied by the Jews since 1967 have organized a concerted programme of resistance known as the Intifada. With its ambushes, selective strikes and small-scale conflicts, the Intifada has effectively demonstrated that occupying the West Bank and Gaza strip is problematic for the Israelis. Beginning in 1992, further peace talks between Israel and Yasser Arafat, the PLO leader, raised hopes that an autonomous Islamic Palestine could be created, committed to peaceful coexistence with Jewish Israel. Only time will tell if this is a realistic vision.

4. JEWISH THOUGHT AFTER THE HOLOCAUST

The Holocaust and the creation of the State of Israel raised enormous theological problems for the Jewish community. Traditionally, the God of Israel has been understood as an all-powerful ruler, who cared for individuals, was profoundly concerned with the destiny of the Jewish people, rewarded the righteous and punished the wicked, and was like a loving spouse and a nurturing parent. How could such a belief be maintained in the face of the gas chambers of Auschwitz and the squalor of Bergen-Belsen? Men, women and children had been herded indiscriminately to their deaths. Even the founding of the State of Israel raised a theological difficulty. The rabbis had taught that the return of the Jewish people to the Promised Land would only occur in the days of the Messiah. When the lion lay down with the lamb and when all twelve tribes were gathered from the corners of the earth, only then would the Temple be rebuilt, the sacrificial system be restored and all nations turn to Jerusalem to learn the ways of the Lord.

Various theologians have wrestled with these problems, but no consensus has emerged. Ignaz Maybaum (1897–1976), a British Reform rabbi, has argued in *The Face of God after Auschwitz* that the suffering of the Jews in the Holocaust was the suffering of God's faithful servant for the sake of humanity. Auschwitz was like Golgotha in the Christian tradition, and the six million victims had purged western civilization so that it could again 'become a place where man can live, do justly, love mercy and walk humbly with God'. Emil Fackenheim (b. 1916) argued that the Holocaust was an expression of God's will that His chosen people must survive. Through the death camps, God issued His 614th commandment 'You shall not grant Hitler a posthumous victory' and, for the sake of Jewish survival, the people of Israel are forbidden to deny or despair of God. Fackenheim believed that the State of Israel is 'collectively what every survivor is individually, a No to the demons of Auschwitz, a Yes to Jewish survival and security and thus a testimony to life against death on behalf of all mankind'. The Orthodox thinker Eliezer Berkovitz (1900–93) argued in *Faith After the Holocaust* that there is no rational explanation for the Holocaust. Jews must simply keep faith in a God who remains silent and whose activities are hidden from human understanding. As he put it, 'Perhaps in the awful misery of man will be revealed to us the awesome mystery of God'. Following the same line, the present author has maintained in *Holocaust Theology* that the destruction of European Jewry can only be understood against a background of divine providence and a belief in life after death.

Other thinkers have given up the struggle. Richard Rubenstein (b. 1924), in *After Auschwitz*, insisted that the Nazi death camps are a decisive refutation of the traditional Jewish belief in a providential God. It is no longer possible to maintain that God has chosen the Jews as His special people or that He takes a special interest in them. It is better to return to ancient Canaanite paganism and positively affirm the value of human life within nature since the God of the Jews is the Ultimate Nothing. Rubenstein has been reviled for his views, but the fact remains that for many Jews, the Holocaust is the final proof of the redundancy of the Jewish religious vision. Rather than confront the possibility of an impotent God who was unable to prevent the horrors of the death camps, or a malevolent God who did not wish to protect His people, it is easier either to forget the whole thing or to identify with the Jewish community solely through a common ethnic background or through financial support for the political State of Israel.

The birth of the State of Israel has proved to be less of a stumbling block. Only among a small group of the ultra-Orthodox has there been a refusal to recognize the new country on the grounds that the days of the Messiah have not yet arrived. In fact, loyalty to the State of Israel has become one of the few factors that unite the Jewish people today, although its creation is not generally perceived as a sign of the imminent coming of the Messiah.

5. THE JEWISH COMMUNITY AFTER WORLD WAR II

The Holocaust and the founding of the State of Israel completely changed the distribution of world Jewry. It is estimated that prior to World War II, Europe contained approximately nine million Jews. By 1945 only three million remained.

Out of a total of thirteen-and-a-half million Jews world-wide, about three-and-a-half million now live in Israel. The United States still has the largest community, with approximately five-and-three-quarter million while over 300,000 live in Canada, 250,000 in Argentina, 130,000 in Brazil and 40,000 in Mexico. After the United States and Israel, the next largest community is that of Russia and the old Soviet states, where the population has been estimated at one-and-three-quarter million. Until very recently, many of these Soviet Jews had little knowledge or understanding of their religious heritage, although their ethnic descent was stamped on their internal passport. A similar situation existed in the Eastern European bloc; Hungary has about 75,000 Jews and Romania about 30,000. The Jewish population of pre-war Poland was about three million but only 200,000 survived, and this number has diminished still further in the years since the war. Altogether in western Europe, there are probably one-and-a-quarter million Jews, with 670,000 in France (many being recent immigrants from North Africa), 360,000 in Great Britain, 42,000 in Germany, 41,000 in Belgium, 35,000 in Italy, 28,000 in the Netherlands and 21,000 in Switzerland. The community of South Africa now numbers about 100,000, with a further 25,000 in North African countries (including the remnants of the black community of Ethiopia). There are also small communities in Iran and Turkey, and tiny ones remain in India and China. The total Jewish population of Australia and New Zealand is approximately 75,000.

The various Jewish populations of Europe have had a complex history since the war. When the concentration camps were liberated, many of the prisoners had no homes to which they could return; their families were dead and the behaviour of their gentile neighbours during the war had given them little cause to hope for a warm welcome. Despite the horrors of the Holocaust, Jews continued to be subject to anti-Semitic attacks in many countries.

The situation in Poland was particularly shocking; many Jews who did go back to their original villages were met with deep hostility by those who had seized their property in their absence. In 1946, an anti-Jewish pogrom in Kielce left forty-two Jews dead, and in direct consequence 5,000 of their co-religionists fled the country and made their way to Palestine. Many others followed their example through the 1950s and 1960s, when there were ferocious government-sponsored anti-Semitic campaigns. Today the Jewish population of Poland is estimated at less than 6,000, the majority of whom are elderly people. Although the Jewish quarter of Krakow is preserved as a historic district, only one synagogue there and one in Warsaw still hold services. Auschwitz itself has become a tourist site, but only recently have the particular sufferings of the Jews been acknowledged there – previously, the victims had been categorized by their nationalities. Poland, the seat of the largest and most vibrant community in Europe, no longer has rabbis, yeshivot, kosher butchers or even facilities for Jewish education.

Initially the survivors of the concentration camps were housed in Displaced Persons' Camps. After the creation of the State of Israel, all limitations on Jewish immigration (except in the case of the chronically sick) were removed, and many of the refugees settled there permanently. Others joined relatives in the United States, Australia and South Africa.

Meanwhile French Jewry became the largest and liveliest community in Europe, with the Ashkenazi survivors being supplemented by an influx of Sephardi newcomers from North Africa. Despite various ugly anti-Semitic incidents, Jewish issues are widely discussed there and a wide range of religious and cultural activity continues. The government of the Netherlands has restored several of the historic synagogues of Amsterdam and there are other small communities in the country. The number of Jews in Germany is small today, but there have been attempts to combat anti-Semitism and to commemorate the victims of the Holocaust. Recently, there has been a revival of interest in the cultural heritage of Spanish Jewry, but the Italian community remains highly assimilated. In Britain, since the country was never occupied by the Nazis, Jewish communal institutions have survived intact. The Chief Rabbi of the United Synagogue is widely respected by Jews and gentiles alike, but the community is deeply divided between the Orthodox and the non-Orthodox, many segments of the population are highly assimilated and rates of intermarriage are high.

In the following chapter, the concerns of today's Jewish community world-wide will be examined in detail.

SUGGESTED FURTHER READING

D. Cohn-Sherbok, *Holocaust Theology*, Lamp, 1989.
L.S. Dawidowicz, *The War Against the Jews 1937–1945*, Holt, Rinehart and Winston, 1975.
L.S. Dawidowicz, ed., *A Holocaust Reader*, Behrman House, 1976.
C.C. O'Brian, *The Siege: The Saga of Israel and Zionism*, Wiedenfeld and Nicolson, 1986.

13 PROBLEMS OF THE JEWISH COMMUNITY TODAY

1. THE PROBLEM OF JEWISH IDENTITY

In any discussion of the state of the Jewish community today, it is vital to define terms. In the past the question of Jewish identity was simple – a person was Jewish if he or she had a Jewish mother or had converted to Judaism. Before the Enlightenment, Judaism was a monolithic system. Jews and gentiles lived apart and only had superficial contact; intermarriage was almost unknown and those who were born, educated, married, and brought up their children in the Jewish tradition had no doubt about their identity. It was only with the breaking down of the ghetto walls that Jewish self-definition become a problem.

In the days of the Spanish Conversos (see Chapter 6, Part 5), Jewishness was understood in religious terms. Once a Jewish family had converted to Christianity, the secular authorities regarded them as no longer Jews – they were free to become full citizens and were subject to the attentions of the Inquisition like their Christian neighbours. Later, anti-Semites had a different view. The Nazis regarded anyone with one Jewish grandparent as being 'non-Aryan', irrespective of their religious belief. Thus there were many in Germany in the 1930s who regarded themselves as practising Christians, and were certainly not accepted as Jews by the Jewish community. Nevertheless they shared the fate of the Jewish people in the Holocaust. A similar situation has arisen in Russia today; because the government understands Jewishness as an ethnic rather than a religious identity, and because all religious teaching has been forbidden for the past seventy years, many Russian Jews have no religious background whatsoever. In addition, many are the products of mixed marriages – their fathers were Jewish, but not their mothers. Such people are not regarded as Jews by the Orthodox establishment, although they have 'Jew' written in their passports and, under the Soviet regime, suffered all the civil disabilities inherent in that status.

The situation is still more complicated in the United States and the countries of the British Commonwealth. Here intermarriage between Jew and gentile is common – probably amounting to fifty per cent of all marriages involving Jews. Moreover, men are more likely to 'marry out' than women, which immediately raises the problem of the status of children. The Reform and Conservative movements (see Part 2) have tried to remedy the situation by encouraging conversion of the non-Jewish spouse. In many American cities, as much as forty per cent of progressive (non-Orthodox) synagogue membership is made up of couples in which one partner has converted. These converted Jews and their children may be accepted as Jews within their own community, but they are not accepted by the Orthodox. Because these people do not even pretend to keep the full halakhah (Jewish law), the Orthodox regard their non-Orthodox conversions as invalid, and insist that they and their children (if it is the woman who has converted) are gentiles.

The Reform movement has taken a different approach. In 1983, their rabbinical association, the Central Conference of American Rabbis, passed a motion that any child of a mixed marriage is 'under presumption of Jewish status'. Even if the gentile mother does not convert, the child is regarded as Jewish provided he or she undergoes 'appropriate and timely public and formal acts of identification with the Jewish faith'. The Orthodox were outraged, but this is now the generally accepted criterion for Reform synagogue membership. Thus in the United States, the home of the biggest Jewish community in the world, many of those who identify themselves as Jews and who belong to synagogues are not regarded as members of the community by many of their co-religionists.

The problem becomes acute with regard to the State of Israel. According to the Law of Return, all Jews have the right to settle in the country and acquire Israeli citizenship, and those who have undergone non-Orthodox conversions are included in this. Although the majority of Israelis are not particularly observant of religious practices, the Orthodox religious parties are constantly demanding that a change be made in the law so that only born-Jews and those converted under

Orthodox supervision may stay. So far this has been resisted, although the Orthodox have complete control of jurisdiction in the courts on matters of personal status. This means that a Reform convert, or the child of a Reform convert, cannot marry in Israel. In addition, many Russian immigrants and even members of some ancient communities such as the Ethiopian are not regarded as fully Jewish; the religious establishment is insisting on Orthodox conversion, to the outrage of many of those involved. Even in the long term, this will not be an easy problem to solve.

2. DIVISIONS WITHIN THE DIASPORA COMMUNITY

The United States has the largest Jewish community in the world, and religious freedom is guaranteed under the American constitution, but only forty-seven per cent of the Jewish population are affiliated to synagogues. The majority of American Jewry have no specific religious affiliation, although they identify in some way as Jews, perhaps in supporting Israel or in affiliating to one of the Jewish communal organizations. In view of this, it is not surprising that intermarriage is common, and in the vast majority of these marriages (where there is no conversion) the children of the marriage do not identify with the community. It is usual to find in the announcements column of any Jewish newspaper that there will be more deaths than births, that most engaged couples will be in their late twenties or early thirties and that, except among the strictly Orthodox, it is unusual to have more than two children. In other words, the American Jewish population is not reproducing itself.

Twenty-three per cent of American Jewish households belong to a Conservative congregation. The Conservative movement originally emerged from the ranks of Reform Judaism (see Chapter 10, Part 3), among those such as Zacharias Frankel who were opposed to radical alterations of the liturgy, and wanted to maintain Sabbath observance and the dietary laws. The movement started in Germany, but a Conservative seminary, the Jewish Theological Seminary, was founded in New York in 1887 and, under the leadership of Solomon Schechter (1847–1915), a body of affiliated synagogues was organized. Today, the Conservative movement continues to uphold the traditionalist position despite subscribing to a critical approach to the Bible. In contrast to Orthodoxy, mixed seating has been introduced, various ritual restrictions have been lifted, and recently women have been ordained as rabbis. This has become the most popular form of religious Judaism in the United States, but it is not accepted by the Orthodox. As far as they are concerned, Conservative rabbis are laymen and Conservative converts are gentiles.

An interesting offshoot of Conservative Judaism is Reconstruction-ism, founded by Mordecai Kaplan (1881–1983). He taught that Judaism should be understood as an evolving religious civilization rather than as a supernaturally revealed religion. The idea is that Reconstructionists are orthodox in practice, but radical in belief. Again, a network of synagogues has been founded with a small but lively group of adherents.

Thirteen per cent of households belong to the Reform movement. American Reform synagogues are known as Temples and the movement is regarded as the most radical and most affluent branch of Judaism. In recent years Reform practices have become more traditional. More Hebrew is used in the services, circumcision for men and immersion in the mikveh (Jewish ritual bath) is increasingly demanded of converts and the movement has almost completely abandoned its anti-Zionist stance. Despite this, it is no more acceptable to the Orthodox than it has ever been. The vast majority of proselytes to Judaism come through the Reform movement, and these conversions remain anathema to the Orthodox.

Nine per cent of the American Jewish population belong to an Orthodox congregation. This is the only branch of American Judaism that is growing. It maintains strict differentiation between the roles of women and men, couples marry very young and contraception is not encouraged. It is not unusual for strictly Orthodox Jewish families to have six or eight children. The movement has founded its own network of schools, yeshivot and seminaries and there is a small but steady stream of baal teshuvah – young people from more progressive backgrounds who have chosen to return to Orthodoxy. There are also various Hasidic groupings all with their own independent institutions. In general, it is true to say that the Orthodox are becoming more rigid in their views and that divisions within the community as a whole are becoming increasingly unbridgeable.

The situation in Great Britain is somewhat different. Here, the main body is the United Synagogue, which appoints the Chief Rabbi and maintains his office. The United Synagogue is moderately Orthodox, and considerably more than half of British Jewry belongs to one of its affiliated synagogues. There are also two more Orthodox organizations which cover four per cent of the Jewish population. The Reform movement is nearer to the American Conservative movement and accounts for thirteen per cent and the Liberals, who are as radical as American Reform, make up seven per cent of British Jewry. The Anglo-Jewish community has the highest level of synagogue affiliation in the Diaspora (eighty-five per cent) and Orthodox membership of eighty per cent. The same pattern is found throughout the British Commonwealth, but everywhere the Jewish population is in decline, with a preponderance of deaths over births.

3. THE SURVIVAL OF THE STATE OF ISRAEL

The only contact of many Jews today with their co-religionists is to be found in their support of the State of Israel. The statement 'We aren't religious, but we do give to Israel' is frequently heard today in assimilated circles. So widespread is this loyalty that American political commentators take it for granted that the 'Jewish vote' will go to the most pro-Israeli candidate, and at election time politicians go out of their way publicly to display their credentials of friendship with Israel. In American Jewish day schools and summer camps, the Israeli flag is commonly displayed with the Stars and Stripes and 'Hatikvah', the Israeli national anthem, is sung with the same patriotic fervour as 'The Star Spangled Banner'. Highly effective support for Israel comes from the Zionist Organization of America and Hadassah, the women's division. The American–Israel Public Affairs Committee, based in Washington, is a lobbying organization applying pressure on Congress, and fundraising is primarily conducted through the United Jewish Appeal. Similar networks of support exist in other countries in the Diaspora.

The Holocaust almost destroyed European Jewry. Once the enormity of the death camps had been discovered, almost all Jewish opposition to the Zionist dream disappeared. The State of Israel was seen to be vital to the survival of the Jewish people. Yet despite the United Nations recommendation in 1947 that there should be an independent Jewish State, the surrounding Arab countries were implacably opposed. The 1948 War of Independence against a superior Arab force helped unite the various Jewish factions, but even after military defeat and international recognition of Israel, the Arab states continued to refuse to accept Israel's existence. The new country was, in effect, in a state of siege. All citizens, female as well as male, were expected to perform a term of military service and to continue training for several years afterwards in the reserves. In the meantime, a flood of new immigrants, particularly Holocaust victims and Sephardim from the surrounding Arab countries, needed to be settled. Houses, schools, colleges, hospitals, clinics and residential homes had to be built; a whole infrastructure needed to be put in place.

The dramatic Israeli victory of the Six Day War in 1967 left the Jews in control of Jerusalem and large tracts of additional territory. It also lost the country much international support. Israel was no longer fighting for its existence, and particularly in the Communist bloc and among left-wing intellectuals, the talk was of Zionist imperialism. This intensified after the Yom Kippur War of 1973. The following year Yasser Arafat, the leader of the Palestine Liberation Organization, was invited to speak to the United Nations and in 1975, the General Assembly passed a resolution equating Zionism with racism.

This had the effect of reinforcing Jewish support for Israel. Nonetheless in 1977, when the Israeli Labour government was superseded by the Likud, led by Menahem Begin (the erstwhile leader of the Irgun, see Chapter 12, Part 3), moderate Zionists felt free to criticize Israeli policies and concern was shown for the Palestinian Arabs. The peace agreement between Israel and Egypt that was achieved in 1979 was a triumph of diplomacy, but the spate of attacks on Jews in the Diaspora by Arab terrorists and neo-Fascists brought home to Jews everywhere the ever-present threat of anti-Semitism. In 1982, the Israeli armed forces invaded Lebanon, officially to root out terrorist bases, and reactions were divided in the Jewish world. Even committed Zionists were perplexed. Those who criticized the invasion were frequently accused of siding with Israel's enemies and being self-hating Jews. Nevertheless there were increasing calls for a just settlement to the Palestinian problem, and even within Israel itself dissent was expressed. The recent peace talks between the Israeli government and the Palestine Liberation Organization about the possibility of a degree of Palestinian autonomy have been widely welcomed.

The relationship between Israel and the Diaspora remains a problem. In the heady days when the State of Israel was first created, many Zionists believed that it was the duty of all Jews to emigrate to Israel, and Israel as a state believed it had the right to speak for the whole of world Jewry. The balance has now shifted. The vast majority of Diaspora Jews support Israel, follow Middle Eastern politics anxiously and, in a real sense, 'pray for the peace of Jerusalem'. Israel provides a powerful common interest and it is a constant focus for pilgrimage, fundraising and education. At the same time, Diaspora Jewry has a life of its own, and most of the Jews living outside Israel will continue to be committed primarily to their own countries and their own communities.

4. RESCUING THREATENED COMMUNITIES

Anti-Semitism did not end with the Holocaust. After the creation of the State of Israel, immigrants arrived not only from the Displaced Persons' Camps of Europe, but also from such ancient communities as those of Iraq (Babylon), Syria and Lebanon. In Iraq in 1920, Jews formed approximately three per cent of the population. Almost all had left by 1958, in response to the tide of Arab nationalism and anti-Zionism. It was the same story in Syria, while the Jews of Lebanon left largely because of economic disruption. For centuries in the Arabian peninsula, Jews had suffered civil disabilities and humiliation. In 1949–50, 44,000 Yemeni and 3,000 Jews from Aden were airlifted to Israel in what was called 'Operation Magic Carpet'. In subsequent years several more thousand left, and now probably only a few hundred remain. Since they had been cut off from the main Jewish centres, they had developed their own customs, many of which they have preserved in Israel. The majority of Turkish Jews have also settled in Israel, as have almost the entire Jewish population of Kurdistan, numbering 30,000 people.

The same pattern appears in North Africa. Although the King of Morocco has repeatedly said that he wants the Moroccan Jewish community to live in peace and security, and Morocco still has the largest Jewish population of any Arab country, it is a remnant compared with the thriving community that existed before the establishment of Israel. In Algeria the Jews found themselves caught between the colonial French and the Arab nationalists. The Great Synagogue of Algiers was raided on Christmas Eve 1960, and this led to the mass emigration of Algerian Jewry. Most settled in France, where they have revitalized the traditional Ashkenazi community. Tunisian independence in 1956 also led to a mass exodus, again mainly to France. The Libyan community has almost entirely settled in Israel, and Egyptian Jewry, particularly harassed after General Nasser seized power and after the Suez campaign of 1956, has mostly emigrated – today, only a few hundred remain.

One community that captured the world's imagination was the Ethiopian. Black Jews have lived in Ethiopia from ancient times; known as the Falashas, they were cut off from mainstream Judaism for centuries and their true origin is not known. Claiming to be descendants of King Solomon and the Queen of Sheba (see Chapter 3, Part 2), they had no knowledge of the Talmud and they had their own unique customs. For many years there was some doubt among the Israeli religious establishment as to whether they really were Jews, but in 1973 the Sephardi Chief Rabbi ruled that they were descendants of the tribe of Dan (see Chapter 3, Part 4), and in 1975 the Israeli government granted them full immigration rights. By 1984 approximately 8,000 Falashas had settled in Israel and that year a further 7,000 were secretly airlifted because of Ethiopian famine and civil war. An estimated 15,000 still remain. Although the Falashas have been accepted, the Orthodox rabbinate has demanded symbolic reconversion to Judaism for those who wish to be married in Israel because of residual doubts about the community's status. This has caused enormous offence and consternation; demonstrations have been held, but as yet no satisfactory agreement has been reached.

The rescue of Soviet Jewry has been another major preoccupation. In common with all citizens of the Soviet Union, Jews were not permitted to travel abroad or to emigrate except in extraordinary circumstances. Anti-Semitism remains a problem in Russia and although numerically Soviet Jewry is the third largest community in the world, it has been subject to a degree of persecution, and religious practice has not been encouraged. Also, increasingly discriminatory quotas were being applied against Jewish candidates for university and the professional schools, and many Jews felt that they and their children could lead fuller lives elsewhere. Applying for an exit visa involved heavy risks; many Jewish activists were condemned to long prison sentences or internal exile, but since 1968 an increasing number of Jews have been allowed to leave for Israel. Numbers varied from year to year, but between 1968 and 1986, more than 266,500 left the Soviet Union.

With the recent liberalization of government, emigration increased still further and has included many prominent dissidents and refuseniks. There is no doubt that the active support of world Jewry for those wishing to emigrate has been an important factor in their release. However, although Israel was the only possible destination for an emigration visa, many of the refuseniks did not wish to go there. More than 100,000 chose to go to the United States after escaping from Russia. Thus, although the issue of Soviet Jewry has been presented as one of religious freedom, in fact many of the emigrants were using their ethnic identification primarily as a means to emigrate to the West. The situation is complicated still further by the fact that many who left are not regarded as Jewish by the Orthodox (see Part 1).

5. JUDAISM AND FEMINISM

Judaism is essentially a patriarchal religion with clearly defined roles for men and women. Although Jewishness is passed on from the female, Jews are described as sons or daughters of their fathers – as in 'Isaac son of Abraham' or 'Dinah daughter of Jacob'. The birth of a son is a matter of great celebration with a ritual circumcision, whereas the birth of a daughter is merely recorded by a baby blessing during the course of a normal synagogue service. After the birth of a son, the mother is regarded as being ritually unclean for fourteen days, but for a daughter the ritual uncleanness lasts for twenty-one. When a boy reaches religious maturity, which is identified as the age of thirteen, he is publicly and ceremoniously called up to read from the Torah Scrolls in the synagogue morning service, and he becomes bar mitzvah (a son of the commandment). Traditionally there was no parallel service for girls and, in any case, there are ritual objections to women even touching the scrolls.

Women are exempt from all time-bound positive commandments and so they are not expected to take an active part in prayer and worship. In the Temple in Jerusalem women were restricted to their own court in an outer area. Today, in Orthodox synagogues they sit apart from the men either behind a heavy screen where they cannot see what is going on or far away above the service in a separate gallery. Neither position encourages direct participation. In any event the Orthodox girl's education has not been directed towards talmudic studies and, because of this, every day in the synagogues the men thank God that they have not been created as women.

Marriage and motherhood are the only acceptable destiny for the Jewish girl. There is no equivalent to the Christian monastic tradition, where a particularly talented woman could develop her own interests and cultivate a private relationship with the Almighty. Women are only revered and remembered as the wives and mothers of great scholars or famous heroes. It has long been the practice for women to work to support the family, leaving the man free from domestic and material cares to practise talmudic scholarship; the wife was created to be a helpmeet for her husband. Turning the pages of the *Encyclopaedia Judaica*, one can find almost no female entries. Through the ages, female Jewish talents have been submerged in a welter of domesticity and child-rearing.

Very little has changed in the strictly Orthodox community. Girls are educated separately from boys, early marriage is encouraged and a large family is regarded as a blessing. Even in Israel, where the equality of men and women is guaranteed in the constitution, strictly Orthodox women are exempt from military service. However, as we have seen, the majority of world Jewry is not particularly observant of religious practices and changing attitudes about the position of women in society have profoundly affected the community.

The complete equality of the sexes has always been an important principle in Reform Judaism. Here women and men sit together in the synagogue and women take a full part in the service. Initially the Reform movement was opposed to bar mitzvah ceremonies, partly because thirteen was thought to be too young and partly because the ostentatious party that all too often accompanied the service was considered undesirable. But popular demand was too strong. Now, among progressive Jews it is usual to have bat mitzvah (daughter of the commandment) services as well as bar mitzvahs. Young girls can show off their Hebrew reading like their brothers, and can enjoy an equally lavish party. In 1972 the first woman Reform rabbi was ordained in the United States, and now it is quite usual in Reform seminaries to have equal numbers of women and men studying for the rabbinate. The Conservative and Reconstructionist movements have followed the Reform example in this and, even among the moderate Orthodox, it is relatively common to have women lay members of the synagogue board.

In the United States and the British Commonwealth, a large proportion of the Jewish community have been to secular universities and have attained high professional qualifications. Like their gentile counterparts, such people are as ambitious for their daughters as for their sons, and large numbers of Jewish young women are studying law, medicine or going to business school. Jews, led by such luminaries as Betty Friedan and Gloria Steinem, have also been very prominent in the feminist movement. Among this highly educated group, late marriage and, at the very most, two children are the norm. Many choose never to marry and find little to attract them in such a family-orientated religious system as Judaism. The strictly Orthodox have met the challenge of modern feminism by ignoring it, but progressive Judaism has taken considerable pains to adapt itself. Nevertheless, for many, the Jewish religious vision remains too patriarchal and too much based on gender role to hold any relevance for modern women and their partners.

SUGGESTED FURTHER READING

G. Abramson, ed., *The Blackwell Companion to Jewish Culture*, Basil Blackwell, 1989.
Nicholas de Lange, *Atlas of the Jewish World*, Phaidon, 1984.
Antony Lerman, ed., *The Jewish Communities of the World*, Macmillan, 1989.
Susan Weidman Schneider, *Jewish and Female*, Simon and Schuster, 1984.

AFTERWORD

What of the future? Some commentators believe that there is no long-term future for the Jewish religion. The birth-rate among Diaspora Jews is too low, they say, and the attractions of assimilation are too great; there will be no more pious Jewish generations. Admittedly the State of Israel probably enjoys a greater measure of security than at any time since its creation, but despite Orthodox control over matters of personal status, Israel is a secular state. The vast majority of Israelis understand their Jewishness as a national rather than as a religious identity. Thus in Israel, as in the Diaspora, this theory maintains, the Jewish faith will only survive among the strictly Orthodox who, despite their many children, will remain an eccentric minority, following their ancient customs, keeping within their own communities and living lives completely out of tune with the manners and mores of the twenty-first century. They will become like the modern Karaites or Samaritans within Judaism, or like the Amish or Mennonites within Christianity – interesting subjects for anthropological theses, but irrelevant to mainstream culture. The more secular-minded of their co-religionists will intermarry with their gentile neighbours, and in common with the Spanish Marranos, they will have dim memories of a Jewish past, but like the Ten Lost Tribes of old, they will ultimately disappear from history.

Other prognoses are not so gloomy, pointing out that Judaism has always adapted itself to changing times and circumstances. The heroes of Masada believed that they were the last of their people, but the scholars of Javneh managed to shake off the trauma of the destruction of the Temple in Jerusalem and to forge a new religious system centred on the synagogue and Torah. Through the mechanism of debate and scholarship, Jewish law adapted itself to changing circumstances. There have been successful communities throughout Europe, America and Asia; they all have had their own individual characteristics, but ultimately they have all accepted the yoke of the covenant. There have always been differences of opinion; the Sadducees quarrelled with the Pharisees, the Rabbanites with the Karaites, the Maimonideans with the anti-Maimonideans, the Shabbeteans with the sceptics and the Hasidim with the Mitnaggdim. But those who support this prognosis emphasize that Judaism has survived, and there is no reason to suppose that things will be any different in the future. Although in each generation some Jews will fall away, enough will remain faithful to Torah and synagogue for the system to survive. Hitler may have decimated the Jews of Europe, but since World War II there has been a revival of Jewish scholarship and the creation of the State of Israel serves as a triumphant rallying point for all. It may be that a greater number of Jews in the future will be more inclined to assert their Jewish identity by supporting Israeli projects than by studying the Talmud, but a firm sense of Jewishness will nonetheless survive down the ages.

There is, however, a radical distinction between the schisms of the past and the split between the Orthodox and the non-Orthodox today. Then, Judaism was essentially a unified structure embracing different interpretations of the meaning of Torah. Today, there is no such common bond. Most Reform and Conservative Jews do not accept the absolute divine authority of the Pentateuch, many Zionists do not even believe in God, and a large proportion of Diaspora Jewry have no religious affiliation whatsoever. Even more serious perhaps is the fact that in two of the three largest Jewish communities, in America and Russia, many of those who identify themselves as Jews are not accepted as such by the Orthodox.

What we are witnessing today is unprecedented fragmentation, and there is very real concern about Jewish identity, whether Jewry is a nation, a religious community or a civilization. The way forward is not clear. On the one hand the progressive movements advocate the adaptation of Jewish law to accommodate the insights of feminism, psychology, sociology and history so that it speaks more harmoniously to the modern human situation. For the Orthodox this is blasphemy. They are adamant that the halakhah is God-given and complete, and that the Torah offers a way of life that is better and nobler than the dishonesty, promiscuity and chaos of secular materialism – it must be cherished and obeyed. From yet a third position, the Zionist argues that only the State of Israel offers a point of allegiance to all Jews, and religious belief has become irrelevant.

The fundamental issue is that of assimilation. Prior to the Enlightenment, Jews had no choice; they were regarded as different by the cultures in which they lived, so they were forced to dwell apart, wear distinctive dress and accept treatment as less than full citizens. In such a context, the Torah served as the only possible basis for a communal life and the rabbis were able to exercise real power within the community. Jews can now make their own choices where they should live, whom they should marry and which profession they should follow. Almost everywhere they have the full benefits and responsibilities of citizenship. Access to secular colleges and universities has caused the influence of the surrounding culture to pervade all aspects of Jewish life.

In a real sense, religious observance has become voluntary. The challenge for the future, then, is to present the faith of Abraham, Isaac and Jacob as sufficiently attractive to retain the allegiance of the Jewish people into the third millennium.

SUGGESTED FURTHER READING

D. Cohn-Sherbok, *Towards the Future of Judaism*, T. and T. Clark, 1994.
Dov Marmur, *Beyond Survival*, Darton Longman and Todd, 1982.
Jonathan Sacks, *One People?*, Littman, 1993.
David Vital, *The Future of the Jews*, Harvard University Press, 1990.

GLOSSARY

ADAM KADMON	Primal man.
AGGADA	Narrative. Rabbinic teachings.
AGUDAT ISRAEL	International organization of Orthodox Jews.
AMISH	American Protestant sect that preserves its old customs.
AMORAIM	Sages whose discussions are recorded in the Gemara.
AMURRU	Ancient nomadic group.
ANTI-SEMITISM	Hatred of the Jewish people.
'APIRU	Ancient nomadic group.
APOCRYPHA	Collection of books written after the books of the Hebrew Bible.
ARK	Main cultic object of the ancient Israelites. The container in the synagogue which holds the scrolls.
ASHKENAZIM	Jews whose ancestors came from Christian Europe.
ASSIMILATION	Absorption into mainstream culture.
AV BET DIN	Vice-president of the ancient Sanhedrin. The president of a rabbinic court.
BAAL TESHUVAH	One who repents and returns to Orthodox Judaism.

BAPTISM	Christian initiation ceremony.
BAR MITZVAH	Thirteen-year-old boy who has taken on the yoke of the Commandments. Coming of age ceremony.
BAT MITZVAH	Twelve-year-old girl who has taken on the yoke of the Commandments. Coming of age ceremony.
BET DIN	Rabbinic Court.
BILU	Russian Zionist youth group.
CALIPH	Islamic ruler.
CANAAN	Ancient name for the Promised Land.
CANAANITES	Ancient inhabitants of the Promised Land.
CANON OF SCRIPTURE	Books which make up the Hebrew Scriptures.
CONSERVATIVE	Modern non-Orthodox denomination within Judaism.
CONVERSOS	Spanish Jews who were compelled to convert to Christianity.
COVENANT	Two-sided agreement.
CRUSADE	Christian military expedition to win back the Holy Land from the Muslims.
DEVEKUT	Cleaving to God.
DIASPORA	Settlement of Jews outside the Promised Land.
DINA MALKHUTA DINA	Rabbinic principle that the law of the land is the law.
DISPERSION	Settlement of Jews outside the Promised Land.
DONMEH	Judeo-Muslim sect formed by followers of Shabbetai Zevi.
EINSATZGRUPPEN	Nazi killing squads.
EIN SOF	The Infinite.
ESSENE	Member of an ancient ascetic sect.
EXILARCH	Head of the Babylonian Jewish community.

FALASHA	Member of the Jewish community of Ethiopia.
GALUT	Exile.
GAON	Head of one of the Babylonian academies.
GEMARA	Discussions of the Mishnah recorded in the Talmud.
GEMATRIA	System of giving numerical value to the Hebrew letters.
GENTILE	A non-Jew.
GHETTO	Area in a city where only Jews could live.
GOLGOTHA	Place of Jesus' crucifixion.
GOYIM	Gentiles.
HAGANAH	Underground Jewish military organization in Palestine.
HALAKHAH	Commandment.
HANUKKAH	Winter festival celebrating the triumph of the Hasmoneans over the Hellenists.
HASIDEI ASHKENAZ	Adherents of a German mediaeval religious movement.
HASID	A pious man. Follower of an 18th-century religious movement.
HASKALAH	The Enlightenment.
HASMONEAN	Descendant of the freedom fighter Simon the Hasmonean.
HATIKVAH	The Hope. The Israeli national anthem.
HELLENIZATION	Ancient movement to spread Greek culture.
HEREM	Excommunication.
HIBBAT ZION	Love of Zion. International Zionist movement.
HISTRADRUT	Israeli federation of trade unions.
HOLOCAUST	The systematic destruction of European Jewry between 1942 and 1945.

HOLY OF HOLIES	Innermost shrine of the Temple in Jerusalem.
INQUISITION	Campaign to root out heresy in the Christian Church in the 16th and 17th centuries.
INTERMARRIAGE	Marriage between Jew and Gentile.
INTIFADA	Palestinian campaign against the Israeli occupying force.
IRGUN	Jewish underground organization in Palestine.
ISRAEL	The Jewish people. The ancient Northern Kingdom of the Jews. An alternative name for the patriarch Jacob. The Jewish nation created in the Middle East in 1948.
ISRAELITES	Ancient nation descended from the patriarch Jacob.
JHWH	The sacred and unpronounceable name of God.
JUDAH	Son of the patriarch Jacob. One of the Twelve Tribes. Ancient Southern Kingdom of the Jews.
JUDEA	Greek name for the Land of Judah.
JUDGES	Ancient charismatic leaders of the Israelites. A book in the Hebrew Scriptures.
KABBALAH	Jewish mystical knowledge.
KARAITE	Adherent of a heretical sect founded by Anan ben David.
KASHRUT	Jewish food laws.
KETUVIM	Writings. Parts of the Hebrew Scriptures that are neither Torah nor prophecy.
KIBBUTZ	Jewish agricultural collective.
KIDDUSH HA-SHEM	Sanctification of God's name. Martyrdom.

K'LAL ISRAEL	The entire Jewish community.
KOHEN	Hereditary priest.
KOLLEL	Advanced Talmudic academy.
KOSHER	Fit to eat according to the Jewish food laws.
LADINO	Language of Sephardic Jewry.
LAW OF RETURN	Israeli law permitting any Jew to immigrate to Israel.
LEVITE	Member of the tribe of Levi. A hereditary priest.
LIKUD	Right-wing Israeli political party.
LOST TRIBES	Ten Israelite tribes who disappeared from history after the Assyrian conquest of 721 BCE.
MAGGID	Preacher.
MAIMONIDEAN	Supporter of the philosopher Maimonides.
MARRANO	Spanish Jew who was forcibly converted to Christianity.
MASHGI'AH	Personal yeshivah counsellor.
MASKIL	Scholar who supported the Haskalah.
MASORETE	Textual scholar of the sixth to ninth centuries.
MATZOS	Unleavened bread eaten at Passover.
MENNONITE	Small Protestant sect that maintains its traditional customs.
MENSCHLIKHEIT	Culture of honourable behaviour.
MERKAVAH	God's chariot as described in the prophecy of Ezekiel.
MESSIAH	Promised Davidic king who will found a reign of peace and justice on earth.
MESSIANIC AGE	A golden era associated with the coming of the Messiah.
MIDRASH	Rabbinic commentary on the Hebrew Scriptures.
MIKVEH	Ritual bath.
MINHAG	Custom.

MINYAN	Quorum of ten men necessary for public prayer.
MISHNAH	Oral Law. The collection of oral law compiled by Judah Ha-Nasi.
MITNAGGDIM	Orthodox scholars who opposed the Hasidim.
MIXED SEATING	Men and women sitting together.
MIZRACHI	Orthodox Zionist organization.
MUSAR	Ethics.
NASI	Prince. President of the Sanhedrin.
NAZI	Supporter of the German National Socialist Party.
NEOLOGISM	Form of Reform Judaism practised in Hungary.
NEO-ORTHODOXY	Modern movement within Orthodoxy.
NEVI'IM	Prophets. Prophetic books of the Hebrew Scriptures.
NORTHERN KINGDOM	Ancient kingdom of Israel.
ORAL LAW	Law discussed by the sages and recorded in the Talmud.
ORTHODOX	In accord with the belief that the written and oral law is of divine origin.
PALESTINE	Name of the Holy Land before it became Israel in 1948.
PASSOVER	Festival celebrating biblical liberation from slavery in Egypt.
PATRIARCHS	Biblical ancestors of the Jews: Abraham, Isaac and Jacob.
PENTATEUCH	First five books of the Hebrew Scriptures.
PHARISEES	Ancient Jewish sect who adhered strictly to the oral law.
PILPUL	Way of interpreting the Talmud that was frequently regarded as over-casuistic.

PIYYUT	Poem.
POALE ZION	Socialist Zionist movement.
POGROM	Violent campaign against the Jews.
PROGRESSIVE	Non-Orthodox.
PROMISED LAND	Land of Canaan promised to the patriarch Abraham.
PROPHET	One who speaks the word of God.
PURIM	Festival commemorating the saving of Persian Jewry by Esther and Mordecai.
QUR'AN	The Muslim holy book.
RABBANITES	Opponents of the Karaites.
RABBI	Ordained Jewish teacher.
RAV	Babylonian title for Jewish scholar.
REBBE	Hasidic leader. Yeshivah teacher.
RECONSTRUCTIONISM	Modern American denomination established by Mordecai Kaplan.
REFORM	Modern non-Orthodox denomination within Judaism.
REFUSENIK	Russian Jew who wishes to settle in Israel.
REICH	German state.
RESPONSA	Answers given by eminent scholars to halakhic questions.
REVISIONISM	Militant Zionist political movement.
SABBATH	Saturday. The seventh day. The day of rest.
SADDUCEES	Hereditary aristocratic priestly party in the days of the Temple.
SAMARITAN	Descendant of the inhabitants of the Northern Kingdom.
SANHEDRIN	Ancient supreme court of the Jews.
SCROLL	Length of parchment on which the Pentateuch or other biblical book is written.
SECOND TEMPLE PERIOD	From 520 BCE – CE 70.
SEFIROT	Emanations from God.

SELIHOT	Penitential prayers.
SELEUCID	King descended from Alexander the Great's general, Seleucus.
SEPHARDIM	Jews who are descended from those who had their origin in Muslim lands.
SEPTUAGINT	Greek translation of the Hebrew Scriptures.
SHABBETEAN	Follower of Shabbetai Zevi.
SHADCHAN	Matchmaker.
SHAVUOT	Festival of the First Fruits, which also celebrates the giving of the Torah.
SHEITEL	Wig.
SHOHET	Kosher slaughterer.
SHTETL	Small Eastern European town largely inhabited by Jews.
SHTIBL	Small meeting place for Hasidic Jews.
SIDDUR	Prayer Book.
SIMHAH	Celebration.
SIMHAT TORAH	Rejoicing in the law. Last day of the festival of Sukkot.
SOUTHERN KINGDOM	Ancient kingdom of Judah.
STREIMEL	Fur hat worn by the Hasidim.
SUFI	Muslim sect.
SUKKOT	Feast of Tabernacles. Autumn harvest festival.
SYNAGOGUE	Meeting place where services are held.
TALLIS	Fringed prayer shawl.
TALMUD	Record of the oral law compiled in Palestine and Babylonia in the fifth and sixth centuries.
TANAKH	Hebrew Bible.
TANNAIM	Sages whose discussions are recorded in the Mishnah.
TEN LOST TRIBES	Inhabitants of the Northern Kingdom who disappeared from history after 721 BCE.
TIKKUN	Repair.

TISHAH B'AV	Day of lamentation for the destruction of the Temple in Jerusalem.
TORAH	Jewish law. The Pentateuch.
TORAH MI-SINAI	Doctrine that the Torah was given in entirety by God to Moses.
TOSAFISTS	French talmudic scholars of the 12th to 14th centuries.
TOSEFTA	Tannaitic work that parallels and supplements the Mishnah.
TRINITY	Christian doctrine that within the Godhead there are three persons.
TSADDIK	Hereditary Hasidic leader.
WISSENSCHAFT DES JUDENTUMS	Scientific study of Judaism.
WORLD ZIONIST ORGANIZATION	International Zionist organization.
WRITTEN LAW	Laws written in the Pentateuch.
YESHIVAH	Talmudic academy.
YIDDISH	Language of Ashkenazi Jewry.
YIDDISHKEIT	Eastern European Jewish culture.
YOM KIPPUR	Day of Atonement.
ZEALOT	Jewish rebel against Rome.
ZIMZUM	Divine emptying.
ZIONISM	International movement dedicated to the return of the Jewish people to the Promised Land.

INDEX